# The Spokesman
## Apocalypse Soon
### Edited by Ken Coates

Published by Spokesman for the
Bertrand Russell Peace Foundation

Spokesman 86                                   2005

## CONTENTS

Editorial  3

The Rise of  7  *Naomi Klein*
Disaster Capitalism

Not Fit to Be  13  *John Humphrys, Tony*
Prime Minister         *Blair, Reg Keys*

Curveball  32  *Charles S Robb &*
                    *Laurence H Silberman*

Iraq and the  41  *Hans von Sponeck*
United Nations

A Sense of Proportion  48  *Ralph Steadman*

Countering  49  *Tony Bunyan*
Civil Rights

Dossier  82  *World Tribunal on Iraq*
                  *Blix on Oil and Iraq War*
                  *Iraq Co-operated*
                  *with Inspectors*
                  *Removing American*
                  *Nuclear Weapons*

Reviews  87  *Ken Coates*
                  *Theresa Wolfwood*
                  *Michael Barratt Brown*
                  *John Pearce*

Cover: The Great Wave off Kanagawa by Katsushika Hokusai
Printed by the Russell Press Ltd., Nottingham, UK

ISSN 0262 7922                          ISBN 0 85124 710 5

**Subscriptions**
Institutions £30.00/€60/$60
Individuals £20.00 (UK)
               £25.00 (ex UK)
               €40/$40

Back issues available on request

A CIP catalogue record for this book is available from the British Library

**Published by the**
Bertrand Russell Peace Foundation Ltd.,
Russell House
Bulwell Lane
Nottingham NG6 0BT
England
Tel. 0115 9784504
email:
elfeuro@compuserve.com
www.spokesmanbooks.com
www.russfound.org

**Editorial Board:**
Michael Barratt Brown
Ken Coates
John Daniels
Ken Fleet
Stuart Holland
Tony Simpson

# RON TODD

*The General Executive Council and Executive Officers of the Transport and General Workers' Union salute the memory of Ron Todd our General Secretary from 1985 to 1992.*

Tony Woodley
General Secretary

Jimmy Kelly
Chair, General
Executive Council

Jack Dromey
Deputy General Secretary

Barry Camfield
Assistant General Secretary

Ray Collins
Assistant General Secretary

Sharon Withers
Executive Finance Director

A trade unionist with unswerving commitment to our movement.

A leader of principle and integrity.

A man of dignity and decency, held in the highest esteem by all who struggled alongside him in the interests of working people.

Today and tomorrow the T&G will remain true to the cause of peace and socialism for which Ron Todd worked.

In sending heartfelt sympathy to Ron's family we share their pride in his life.

tel: 020 7611 2500    www.tgwu.org.uk    fax: 020 7611 2555

# Editorial

# Apocalypse Soon

The headlines were quite abnormally ambivalent. Saluting the 2005 Election result in Britain, *The Independent* newspaper shouted *'Eight years on, why does victory feel like defeat?'*

Actually, the Blair administration secured a majority in Parliament of sixty-seven, or, perhaps ultimately, sixty-six. Not to quibble, this was definitely a win. The British political balance has often been narrower. But winning what? The electoral turn-out has almost never been lower, and the large preponderance of Labour Members in the House of Commons was based only on the votes of twenty-two per cent of the British people. Mass abstention was the visible outcome of recent political processes. But beneath the public view there had been a consistent erosion of activism in which the Labour Party suffered particularly severely. In large parts of the country, there were no willing proselytes to carry messages, deliver leaflets and knock on doors. The old language persists, in which candidates speak of the news they received 'on the doorstep'. But the number of doorsteps that have actually been stood upon by politicians' feet must in this contest have hit an all-time low.

Insofar as Labour candidates voyaged out into the very rough seas of present public opinion, they gathered messages which were far from welcome to their leaders. The war in Iraq was deeply unpopular. But in fact, it was even more unpopular in the British establishment than it was among the common people. The intelligence establishment was particularly scandalised, and demonstrated its reactions by maintaining a constant and debilitating flow of embarrassing leaks, which showed how thoroughly baseless was the official case for war, and how remote was official propaganda from any conceivable relationship with the truth. The fourth estate was almost equally disenchanted, with the result that all kinds of opinions received a hearing more normally filtered out by discreet blankets of censorship. So distressed was the established church that some dignitaries spoke directly for candidates who were opposing the Prime Minister in his own Constituency.

The result will, if anything, prove to have been more turbulent than the voting in the Election itself. Be sure, there is no rational justification for Britain's continuing participation in the Iraqi occupation. However the withdrawal is ultimately arranged, there is little doubt that it has arrived firmly on the immediate agenda. However the departure of Mr. Blair is finessed, there is also little doubt that Mrs. Blair will soon be preoccupied with the décor of her fine new house in Millionaires' Row.

All these things will surely help to shape the political agenda in Britain, at any rate, in the post-Election period.

But there is another item which should be on that agenda, and which desperately needs our attention. This concerns the

> 'reliance on nuclear weapons as a foreign policy tool ... Current US nuclear weapons policy (is) immoral, illegal, militarily unnecessary, and dreadfully dangerous. The risk of an accidental or inadvertent nuclear launch is unacceptably high. Far from reducing these risks the Bush administration has signalled that it is committed to keeping the US nuclear arsenal as a mainstay of this military power – a commitment that is simultaneously eroding the international norms that have limited the spread of nuclear weapons and fissile materials for fifty years.'

These are the words of Robert S. McNamara, the American Secretary of Defence from 1961 to 1968. He should know:

> 'Much of the current US nuclear policy has been in place since before I was Secretary of Defence, and it has only grown more dangerous and diplomatically destructive in the intervening years.'

McNamara's article in the American journal *Foreign Policy* carries the title 'Apocalypse Soon'.

There is, of course, more than one road to apocalypse. Tony Blair seeks to embroil Britain in travelling its own way, alongside his patron.

On the 2nd of May 2005, *The Independent* reported:

> 'Tony Blair has secretly decided that Britain will build a new generation of nuclear deterrent to replace the ageing Trident submarine fleet at a cost of more than £10bn – a move certain to dismay thousands of Labour Party loyalists in the approach to polling day.
>
> The disclosure that the decision has already been taken will expose Mr. Blair – who has struggled throughout the election campaign to fend off accusations that he lied over the Iraq war – to fresh allegations of deception. He said last week that the decision would be taken after 5th May.
>
> But *The Independent* has learnt that he has already decided to give the go ahead for a replacement for Trident to stop Britain surrendering its status as a nuclear power when the Trident fleet is decommissioned. The choice over the type of nuclear missile system that Britain will deploy is yet to be made. One Labour candidate described the new deterrent as "Blair's weapons of mass destruction".
>
> The revelation comes as the United Nations hosts a five-yearly review of the Nuclear Non-proliferation Treaty, to which Britain is a signatory. The five nuclear powers in the Treaty promise to work towards global nuclear disarmament. Mr. Blair will therefore face accusations of hypocrisy ...'

The renewal of the British so-called deterrent does not have any justification in coherent military doctrine, still less in global nuclear policy. Trident submarines hold no terrors for Osama bin Laden, whose weapon of choice is the Stanley knife. But by reinforcing the old stereotypes, behaving as if the Cold War could still justify all foreign policy, when in fact we now inhabit a different universe, British and American leaders run the risk of creating the very explosion which they claim they would like to deter.

The current round of negotiations on the non-proliferation regime, in New

York, is already overshadowed by arguments about Iranian and Korean nuclear proliferation. But the truth is that the proliferation of weapons can never be understood, still less reversed, without addressing the power imbalances which have given rise to it. Why should the Iranian bomb be more frightening than the Pakistani bomb? The objections to both are very similar in that they deprive their peoples of resources that could be better deployed on other projects. But the motor of the Iranian bomb, if such there be, must clearly be seen in Israel where there is a regime armed to its nuclear teeth, which clearly poses a threat to the Iranians. And what protection will the Israeli deterrent offer to the people in Tel Aviv, if the touch paper in the Middle East is ever lit?

Ultimately the American policy remains very simple: to browbeat and intimidate all those who do not willingly follow the instructions of the imperial power. But these instructions are numerous and widely diffused, issued almost at random. Their very extension only serves to bring nearer the day when someone will defy them.

Reliance on 4,500 strategic nuclear warheads in the United States, and 3,800 in Russia, is no less ridiculous than dependence on an estimated two to eight such bombs in Korea. The bombs will be likely to destroy those who depend upon them, unless rationality supervenes.

*Ken Coates*

# The Collected Works of Marx and Engels
## Save £750 on the complete 50 volume set

The publication of the definitive English language edition of the *Collected Works of Marx and Engels*, in 50 volumes, was completed this year, when the last volume was released. The series contains all the works of Marx and Engels, whether published during their lifetimes or since, and includes their complete correspondence as well as many works previously unpublished in English.

To mark the completion of this long term project, Lawrence and Wishart is making a **special offer** for the whole set. Each volume normally costs £45, making the cost of 50 volumes £2,250. But you can pay now and get the whole set for just £1,500 post free (UK orders only, overseas p&p £150).

To take advantage of this offer, simply send your cheque or Visa/MasterCard details to Lawrence and Wishart, PO Box 7701, Latchingdon, Chelmsford, CM3 6WL or visit our website for more information. You can also pay for and receive your volumes in instalments – for more information contact the L&W office.

'*Indispensable to anyone with a serious interest in Marx, Marxism and the nineteenth century ... It is unlikely that this edition of the Collected Works will ever need to be replaced.*'
**E. J. Hobsbawm**

'*The series still represents at least twice the value for money of any comparable product on offer elsewhere. Not only does it maintain a consistently good standard of production, it is beautifully indexed and presented.*' **Ken Coates, Tribune**

# BERTRAND RUSSELL

Get inside one of the greatest minds of the 20th Century

'There is no one who uses the English language more beguilingly than Russell, no one smoothes the kinks and creases more artfully out of the most crumpled weaves of thought.' – *The Times*

## ABC of Relativity
**Bertrand Russell**
Introduction by **Peter Clark**

Bertrand Russell's most brilliant work of scientific popularisation.

Pb: 0-415-15429-4: £11.99

## The Scientific Outlook
**Bertrand Russell**

This early classic illuminates Russell's thinking on the promise and threat of scientific progress.

Hb: 0-415-24996-1: £50.00
Pb: 0-415-24997-X: £13.99

## The Collected Papers of Bertrand Russell Volume 29
*NEW*
Détente or Destruction, 1955-57
**Bertrand Russell**
Edited by **Andrew G. Bone**

Continues the publication of Routledge's multi-volume critical edition of Bertrand Russell's shorter writings.

February 2005
Hb: 0-415-35837-X: £125.00

## Common Sense and Nuclear Warfare
**Bertrand Russell**
Introduction by **Ken Coates**

This book presents Russell's keen insights into the threat of nuclear conflict, and his argument that the only way to end this threat is to end war itself.

Hb: 0415249945: £50.00
Pb: 0415249953: £9.99

## Power
A New Social Analysis
**Bertrand Russell**
Introduction by **Samuel Brittan**

In this remarkable book Russell argues that power is man's ultimate goal and is, in its many guises, the single most important element in the development of any society.

*Routledge Classics series*
Pb: 0-415-32507-2: £9.99

For details on our full range of Bertrand Russell titles, and how to order, please visit
**www.routledge.com**

For credit card orders: call +44 (0)1264 343071
or email book.orders@routledge.co.uk
For more information, or for a free Philosophy catalogue please call
Helen Lawton on 020 7017 6044 or email helen.lawton@tandf.co.uk

Routledge
Taylor & Francis Group

# The Rise of Disaster Capitalism

*Naomi Klein*

Naomi Klein is the author of No Logo *and writer/producer of* The Take, *a documentary about Argentina's occupied factories.*

Last summer, in the lull of the August media doze, the Bush Administration's doctrine of preventive war took a major leap forward. On 5 August 2004, the White House created the Office of the Coordinator for Reconstruction and Stabilization, headed by former US Ambassador to Ukraine Carlos Pascual. Its mandate is to draw up elaborate 'post-conflict' plans for up to twenty-five countries that are not, as of yet, in conflict. According to Pascual, it will also be able to coordinate three full-scale reconstruction operations in different countries 'at the same time,' each lasting 'five to seven years.'

Fittingly, a government devoted to perpetual pre-emptive deconstruction now has a standing office of perpetual pre-emptive reconstruction.

Gone are the days of waiting for wars to break out and then drawing up *ad hoc* plans to pick up the pieces. In close cooperation with the National Intelligence Council, Pascual's office keeps 'high risk' countries on a 'watch list' and assembles rapid-response teams ready to engage in pre-war planning and to 'mobilise and deploy quickly' after a conflict has gone down. The teams are made up of private companies, non-governmental organisations and members of think tanks – some, Pascual told an audience at the Centre for Strategic and International Studies in October, will have 'pre-completed' contracts to rebuild countries that are not yet broken. Doing this paperwork in advance could 'cut off three to six months in your response time.'

The plans Pascual's teams have been drawing up in his little-known office in the State Department are about changing 'the very social fabric of a nation,' he told CSIS. The office's mandate is not to rebuild any old states, you see, but to create 'democratic and market-oriented' ones. So, for instance (and he was just pulling this example out of his hat, no doubt), his fast-acting reconstructors might help sell off 'state-owned enterprises that created a nonviable economy.' Sometimes rebuilding, he explained, means 'tearing apart the old.'

Few ideologues can resist the allure of a blank slate – that was colonialism's seductive promise: 'discovering' wide-open new lands where utopia seemed possible. But colonialism is dead, or so we are told; there are no new places to discover, no *terra nullius* (there never was), no more blank pages on which, as Mao once said, 'the newest and most beautiful words can be written.' There is, however, plenty of destruction – countries smashed to rubble, whether by so-called Acts of God or by Acts of Bush (on orders from God). And where there is destruction there is reconstruction, a chance to grab hold of 'the terrible barrenness,' as a UN official recently described the devastation in Aceh, and fill it with the most perfect, beautiful plans.

'We used to have vulgar colonialism,' says Shalmali Guttal, a Bangalore-based researcher with Focus on the Global South. 'Now we have sophisticated colonialism, and they call it "reconstruction."'

It certainly seems that ever-larger portions of the globe are under active reconstruction: being rebuilt by a parallel government made up of a familiar cast of for-profit consulting firms, engineering companies, mega-NGOs, government and UN aid agencies and international financial institutions. And from the people living in these reconstruction sites – Iraq to Aceh, Afghanistan to Haiti – a similar chorus of complaints can be heard. The work is far too slow, if it is happening at all. Foreign consultants live high on cost-plus expense accounts and thousand-dollar-a-day salaries, while locals are shut out of much-needed jobs, training and decision-making. Expert 'democracy builders' lecture governments on the importance of transparency and 'good governance,' yet most contractors and non-governmental organisations refuse to open their books to those same governments, let alone give them control over how their aid money is spent.

Three months after the tsunami hit Aceh, the *New York Times* ran a distressing story reporting that 'almost nothing seems to have been done to begin repairs and rebuilding.' The dispatch could easily have come from Iraq, where, as the *Los Angeles Times* just reported, all of Bechtel's allegedly rebuilt water plants have started to break down, one more in an endless litany of reconstruction screw-ups. It could also have come from Afghanistan, where President Hamid Karzai recently blasted 'corrupt, wasteful and unaccountable' foreign contractors for 'squandering the precious resources that Afghanistan received in aid.' Or from Sri Lanka, where 600,000 people who lost their homes in the tsunami are still languishing in temporary camps. One hundred days after the giant waves hit, Herman Kumara, head of the National Fisheries Solidarity Movement in Negombo, Sri Lanka, sent out a desperate e-mail to colleagues around the world. 'The funds received for the benefit of the victims are directed to the benefit of the privileged few, not to the real victims,' he wrote. 'Our voices are not heard and not allowed to be voiced.'

But if the reconstruction industry is stunningly inept at rebuilding, that may be because rebuilding is not its primary purpose. According to Guttal, 'It's not reconstruction at all – it's about reshaping everything.' If anything, the stories of corruption and incompetence serve to mask this deeper scandal: the rise of a predatory form of disaster capitalism that uses the desperation and fear created by catastrophe to engage in radical social and economic engineering. And on this front, the reconstruction industry works so quickly and efficiently that the privatisations and land grabs are usually locked in before the local population knows what hit them. Kumara, in another e-mail, warns that Sri Lanka is now facing 'a second tsunami of corporate globalisation and militarisation,' potentially even more devastating than the first. 'We see this as a plan of action amidst the tsunami crisis to hand over the sea and the coast to foreign corporations and tourism, with military assistance from the US Marines.'

As Deputy Defence Secretary, Paul Wolfowitz designed and oversaw a strikingly similar project in Iraq: the fires were still burning in Baghdad when US occupation officials rewrote the investment laws and announced that the country's state-owned companies would be privatised. Some have pointed to this track record to argue that Wolfowitz is unfit to lead the World Bank; in fact, nothing could have prepared him better for his new job. In Iraq, Wolfowitz was just doing what the World Bank is already doing in virtually every war-torn and disaster-struck country in the world – albeit with fewer bureaucratic niceties and more ideological bravado.

'Post-conflict' countries now receive 20-25 per cent of the World Bank's total lending, up from 16 per cent in 1998 – itself an 800 percent increase since 1980, according to a Congressional Research Service study. Rapid response to wars and natural disasters has traditionally been the domain of United Nations agencies, which worked with non-governmental organisations to provide emergency aid, build temporary housing and the like. But now reconstruction work has been revealed as a tremendously lucrative industry, too important to be left to the do-gooders at the UN. So today it is the World Bank, already devoted to the principle of poverty-alleviation through profit-making, that leads the charge.

And there is no doubt that there are profits to be made in the reconstruction business. There are massive engineering and supplies contracts ($10 billion to Halliburton in Iraq and Afghanistan alone); 'democracy building' has exploded into a $2 billion industry; and times have never been better for public-sector consultants – the private firms that advise governments on selling off their assets, often running government services themselves as subcontractors. (Bearing Point, the favoured of these firms in the United States, reported that the revenues for its 'public services' division 'had quadrupled in just five years,' and the profits are huge: $342 million in 2002 – a profit margin of 35 percent.)

But shattered countries are attractive to the World Bank for another reason: they take orders well. After a cataclysmic event, governments will usually do whatever it takes to get aid dollars – even if it means racking up huge debts and agreeing to sweeping policy reforms. And with the local population struggling to find shelter and food, political organising against privatisation can seem like an unimaginable luxury.

Even better from the bank's perspective, many war-ravaged countries are in states of 'limited sovereignty': they are considered too unstable and unskilled to manage the aid money pouring in, so it is often put in a trust fund managed by the World Bank. This is the case in East Timor, where the bank doles out money to the government as long as it shows it is spending responsibly. Apparently, this means slashing public-sector jobs (Timor's government is half the size it was under Indonesian occupation) but lavishing aid money on foreign consultants the bank insists the government hire (researcher Ben Moxham writes, 'In one government department, a single international consultant earns in one month the same as his twenty Timorese colleagues earn together in an entire year').

In Afghanistan, where the World Bank also administers the country's aid through a trust fund, it has already managed to privatise healthcare by refusing to give funds to the Ministry of Health to build hospitals. Instead it funnels money directly to non-governmental organisations, which are running their own private health clinics on three-year contracts. It has also mandated 'an increased role for the private sector' in the water system, telecommunications, oil, gas and mining and directed the government to 'withdraw' from the electricity sector and leave it to 'foreign private investors.' These profound transformations of Afghan society were never debated or reported on, because few outside the bank know they took place: the changes were buried deep in a 'technical annexe' attached to a grant providing 'emergency' aid to Afghanistan's war-torn infrastructure – two years before the country had an elected government.

It has been much the same story in Haiti, following the ouster of President Jean-Bertrand Aristide. In exchange for a $61 million loan, the bank is requiring 'public-private partnership and governance in the education and health sectors,' according to bank documents – i.e., private companies running schools and hospitals. Roger Noriega, US Assistant Secretary of State for Western Hemisphere Affairs, has made it clear that the Bush Administration shares these goals. 'We will also encourage the government of Haiti to move forward, at the appropriate time, with restructuring and privatisation of some public sector enterprises,' he told the American Enterprise Institute on April 14, 2004.

These are extraordinarily controversial plans in a country with a powerful socialist base, and the bank admits that this is precisely why it is pushing them now, with Haiti under what approaches military rule. 'The Transitional Government provide[s] a window of opportunity for implementing economic governance reforms...that may be hard for a future government to undo,' the bank notes in its Economic Governance Reform Operation Project agreement. For Haitians, this is a particularly bitter irony: many blame multilateral institutions, including the World Bank, for deepening the political crisis that led to Aristide's ouster by withholding hundreds of millions in promised loans. At the time, the Inter-American Development Bank, under pressure from the State Department, claimed Haiti was insufficiently democratic to receive the money, pointing to minor irregularities in a legislative election. But now that Aristide is out, the World Bank is openly celebrating the perks of operating in a democracy-free zone.

The World Bank and the International Monetary Fund have been imposing shock therapy on countries in various states of shock for at least three decades, most notably after Latin America's military coups and the collapse of the Soviet Union. Yet many observers say that today's disaster capitalism really hit its stride with Hurricane Mitch. For a week in October 1998, Mitch parked itself over Central America, swallowing villages whole and killing more than 9,000. Already impoverished countries were desperate for reconstruction aid – and it came, but with strings attached. In the two months after Mitch struck, with the country still knee-deep in rubble, corpses and mud, the Honduran congress initiated what the *Financial Times* called 'speed sell-offs after the storm.' It passed laws allowing the privatisation of airports, seaports and highways and fast-tracked plans to privatise the state telephone company, the national electric company and parts of the water sector. It overturned land-reform laws and made it easier for foreigners to buy and sell property. It was much the same in neighbouring countries: in the same two months, Guatemala announced plans to sell off its phone system, and Nicaragua did likewise, along with its electric company and its petroleum sector.

All of the privatisation plans were pushed aggressively by the usual suspects. According to the *Wall Street Journal*, 'the World Bank and International Monetary Fund had thrown their weight behind the [telecom] sale, making it a condition for release of roughly $47 million in aid annually over three years and linking it to about $4.4 billion in foreign-debt relief for Nicaragua.'

Now the bank is using the December 26 tsunami to push through its cookie-cutter policies. The most devastated countries have seen almost no debt relief, and most of the World Bank's emergency aid has come in the form of loans, not grants. Rather than emphasising the need to help the small fishing communities – more than 80 per cent of the wave's victims – the bank is pushing for expansion of the tourism sector and industrial fish farms. As for the damaged public infrastructure, like roads and schools, bank documents recognise that rebuilding them 'may strain public finances' and suggest that governments consider privatisation (yes, they have only one idea). 'For certain investments,' notes the bank's tsunami-response plan, 'it may be appropriate to utilise private financing.'

As in other reconstruction sites, from Haiti to Iraq, tsunami relief has little to do with recovering what was lost. Although hotels and industry have already started reconstructing on the coast, in Sri Lanka, Thailand, Indonesia and India, governments have passed laws preventing families from rebuilding their oceanfront homes. Hundreds of thousands of people are being forcibly relocated inland, to military style barracks in Aceh and prefab concrete boxes in Thailand. The coast is not being rebuilt as it was – dotted with fishing villages and beaches strewn with handmade nets. Instead, governments, corporations and foreign donors are teaming up to rebuild it as they would like it to be: the beaches as playgrounds for tourists, the oceans as watery mines for corporate fishing fleets, both serviced by privatised airports and highways built on borrowed money.

In January Condoleezza Rice sparked a small controversy by describing the tsunami as 'a wonderful opportunity' that 'has paid great dividends for us.' Many were horrified at the idea of treating a massive human tragedy as a chance to seek advantage. But, if anything, Rice was understating the case. A group calling itself

Thailand Tsunami Survivors and Supporters says that for 'businessmen-politicians, the tsunami was the answer to their prayers, since it literally wiped these coastal areas clean of the communities which had previously stood in the way of their plans for resorts, hotels, casinos and shrimp farms. To them, all these coastal areas are now open land!'

Disaster, it seems, is the new *terra nullius*.

© Copyright Naomi Klein 2005

With grateful acknowledgements to *The Nation* (www.thenation.com)

---

## Arguments Against G8
Edited by Gill Hubbard and David Miller
With Noam Chomsky • Susan George • Mark Curtis • George Monbiot • Caroline Lucas, MEP

"One of the most important books in recent years. .... I cannot recommend it highly enough." Robert W. McChesney, author, *The Problem with the Media*

"This book reminds us brilliantly that, far from ending poverty, today's political elites are the chief creators of human want, war and ecological disaster." John McAllion, Oxfam Scotland

Published by Pluto Press • May 2005 • Pb • £11.99 • 0 7453 2420 7

## Ecological Debt
*The Health of the Planet and the Wealth of Nations*
Andrew Simms

"Never has the idea of 'living beyond your means' seemed so terrifying and potentially disastrous. This book shows that we're in-the-red like we never knew. Forget your bank balance, now we're all going to be talking about ecological debt. A new phrase has entered the language." Anita Roddick, founder of The Body Shop

Published by Pluto Press • May 2005 • Pb • £12.99 • 0 7453 2404 5

PLUTO PRESS
Independent Progressive Publishing
www.plutobooks.com

# Not Fit To Be Prime Minister

*John Humphrys*
*Tony Blair*
*Reg Keys*

*There continues a strenuous campaign to hold Prime Minister Blair to account for taking the United Kingdom to war against Iraq. This four-part dossier reflects aspects of that campaign, concluding with the call by the families of soldiers killed in Iraq for a full Public Inquiry into the legality of the war in which their relatives died.*

## I

*On the 29th September 2004, Tony Blair gave an interview to John Humphrys on the BBC Radio 4 morning programme Today. This was very revealing, and it deserves to be borne in mind when evaluating the decision to launch a war, and the consequences of that decision.*

*Whilst the interview itself is lucid, there are a number of issues which arise out of the Prime Minister's statements. Of course, new evidence continues to appear. But John Humphrys' questions were entirely pertinent, and he succeeded in going to the heart of the matter.*

*This text was transcribed by Tony Simpson, and Ken Coates wrote the commentary.*

\* \* \*

We should refresh our memories about the true costs of this war, which is now presented as the righteous overthrow of Saddam Hussein. But it was far more than a passive coup d'état. This illegal war had disastrous consequences for Iraqi civilians, some one hundred thousand of whom have been killed. 'It is estimated that ninety-eight thousand more deaths than expected happened after the invasion, outside of Falluja, and far more if the Falluja cluster is included', reported *The Lancet* in their comprehensive survey of civilian mortality in Iraq.[1]

*The Lancet* made extremely careful estimates of the death toll, and if anything, the numbers they have recorded will prove to have been underestimates. This death toll does not include the figures of military casualties. The coalition, contrary to the Geneva Conventions, did not record the numbers of dead and wounded among the Iraqi military, leave alone civilian deaths, although, of course, such numbers were recorded where they involved soldiers of the coalition itself. Article 27 of the Fourth Geneva Convention says that civilians 'shall at all times be humanely treated, and shall be protected especially against acts of violence'. But *The Lancet* estimate states that more than half the civilian deaths caused by the occupying forces *were women and children*.

It is arguable that the reduction of Falluja constituted a war crime, in which the American forces were abetted by Britain, which made special deployments from the Black Watch in order to provide cover for the Americans.

It is in this horrific context that we should now judge the arcane arguments about Iraqi weapons of mass destruction, which the world now knows never existed. There follows the text of the Humphrys' radio interview.

## John Humphrys talks to Tony Blair
### The Today Programme, 29.9.2004

***JH:*** *If Tony Blair now accepted that there were no weapons of mass destruction, why didn't he accept that we had been taken to war on a false prospectus?*

**TB:** The difficulty I have is this. I can apologise for the fact that the information we gave has turned out to be wrong. I've maintained very strongly that it was given in good faith, and shared by most other people. The trouble is, I can't apologise for saying that we got rid of Saddam Hussein, or that the basis on which we went to war was wrong, because we took the action as a result of Saddam's failure to comply with UN resolutions. That non-compliance still stands.

***JH:*** *We did not go to war, or we were not told we were going to war, to get rid of Saddam Hussein.*

**TB:** That's absolutely right. Regime change was not the cause for it. The cause for it was that — what I did was take the view after September 11 that we had to take a totally new approach. And what that meant is that in respect of regimes developing weapons of mass destruction, instead of taking a reactive approach, we had to take an active approach. Therefore, the place to start was Iraq, because there was a string of UN resolutions, a long history of UN inspections not working, and so we went back to the United Nations, got a fresh resolution, which said that he had to comply fully with the UN inspection regime. Now, in the end, he didn't, so that was the legal basis for the war. The regime, as I think I said, actually, before the war began, the regime was not irrelevant because, of course, the possibility of weapons of mass destruction in the hands of a malign regime is different from that if they're in the hands of a benign regime…

***JH:*** *You were very clear when you said I've never put the justification for action as regime change.*

**TB:** Yes, absolutely.

***JH:*** *But in the end that's what happened.*

**TB:** What happened was we got rid of the regime, because that was the only way that…

**JH:** *A regime that was not threatening us.*

**TB:** Well, I don't accept that. I don't accept that they weren't a threat, because the issue was, were they in compliance with UN resolutions?

**JH:** *Was that the issue, or were they a threat? Because when you told us that you wanted to go to war in Iraq, you did so because they were a threat to us. That surely can be the only reason why a Prime Minister takes a country to war?*

**TB:** Of course, but the nature of the threat was that, because of the UN resolutions that had been passed in respect of Iraq, which we then got renewed in the resolution in November 2002, and that resolution said that Saddam had to comply fully and unconditionally with the UN inspectors. He wasn't doing so. So in the end we were faced with a situation. Let's be clear, the only reason the UN inspectors were back in Iraq at all was because we had 200,000 American and British troops down there. Now, we couldn't leave them there forever, so we had to come to a point. We did so in November 2002. The resolution was passed saying he had to comply fully, unconditionally, completely, and he didn't.

**JH:** *It wasn't a resolution, according to the Secretary General of the United Nations and the Security Council, that justified war. In the view of the Secretary General the war was not legal. He made that very clear last month.*

**TB:** That is his view. It's not our view.

**JH:** *It's the view of the man who runs the only legal organisation that we have of its kind to which we subscribe.*

**TB:** I'm afraid we took the view, we took it at the time, we take it now, that the war was justified legally because he remained in breach of the UN resolutions. The issue, I think, I haven't in fact studied the actual words that Kofi used, but I think the issue he was talking about was whether the resolution 1441 — we can go back into the detail — was such that it would actually justify action if there was a breach of it. I don't think he or anybody else is disputing that there was, indeed, a breach of resolution 1441.

**JH:** *'I have made it clear that it was not in conformity, the decision to go to war, with the Security Council, with the UN Charter.' 'It was illegal?' 'Yes, it was illegal.' That's what he said.*

**TB:** I totally understand that, and I'm not disputing it. I'm simply saying that we don't accept that. We believe it was, and the reason we believe it was, is that we believe if there was a breach of resolution 1441, then we were justified in taking military action.

**JH:** *What you said yesterday was that you apologised for the information, the intelligence information you had, being wrong. What puzzles many people about that is that you seem to have accepted that information in a very naïve, in fact gullible, way, and the reason for that, and people like Robin Cook suggest this, don't they, is that you had already decided with President Bush that you would go to war? So you were not looking for information that would prove the case for war. You were looking for information that would justify a decision you had already reached.*

**TB:** I entirely agree that's what people say. Now let me deal with the two aspects of it. The first is that, somehow, this information really wasn't of any importance at all. The fact is, as I indicated when I spoke to the House of Commons, and actually went through, not the so-called 'Dossier', but went through the intelligence itself. There was no doubt in respect of the intelligence about Saddam and weapons of mass destruction. That was absolutely clear. So it wasn't a question of being naïve or gullible. The intelligence we had was intelligence I believe that any sensible, reasonable Prime Minister would say 'That's clear evidence there is a WMD threat here.' In respect of the second part, it simply is not correct. Let me just tell you something. When we first had the discussions about this, myself and President Bush, in the course of 2002, our case was this is an issue we have to deal with post 9/11. Of course, it never was the case that Saddam was about to launch an attack on Britain or the United States, but we had to go back and start enforcing the UN resolutions in respect of weapons of mass destruction, and take a completely different stand. Why? Because of our fear that if terrorists ever got hold of these weapons, the destruction they would wreak would be massive and devastating in the consequences of them. When we then decided to go back to the United Nations, had Saddam complied fully with the UN resolution, there wouldn't have been a conflict. It may well be a good idea, and it is a good idea, that Saddam is out of power, but the fact is that at the time, we accepted fully the justification was his failure to comply with UN resolutions. Now, we believe, and I believe now, I think it's the reason why it has passed virtually without comment, that a couple of weeks ago Libya finally wound up its weapons of mass destruction programme. America's lifted sanctions. We've got a better chance of getting Iran and North Korea into compliance than we have ever had. I thought, and I still think, that it was absolutely essential that we took that stand.

**JH:** *Let me come back to that. You say that there was no doubt about that evidence. There was doubt. There was considerable doubt about it. I spoke myself, and others did too, to very senior figures in intelligence who said, and I quote on the basis of one particular conversation, on any Cartesian analysis 'Iraq does not emerge as the priority. There were other priorities: Syria and Iran, perhaps.' There were questions about the 45 minute warning.*

**TB:** John, could I just interrupt you a minute there? I think it's very important to realise why it is we went in respect of Iraq, first. The reason was – I'm not saying there aren't weapons of mass destruction issues about Iran or North Korea, for example. There certainly are. But the reason we went to Iraq, the reason I thought it was right to start with Iraq in respect of this issue, was the long history of the country that had actually used weapons of mass destruction, that had then, for four years in the early 1990s, you'd had inspectors in Iraq not finding weapons of mass destruction.

*JH: Yes, but they weren't regarded as a threat. That's the point. The 45 minute threat, in particular, which you appeared to be unaware of, that is to say you were confused as to whether it was battlefield or longer-range weapons, baffled many people. Why didn't you ask the questions? Unless you were so keen, so enthusiastic about going to war because George Bush wanted you to go to war, why did you not ask the sorts of questions that would have revealed the information you needed to say 'Hang on a minute. Maybe this isn't the right thing to do'?*

**TB:** First of all, the information that he was still intent on developing weapons of mass destruction and had actually readily deployable weapons, that was nothing to do with the 45 minutes. There was a mass of evidence to that effect, a mass of intelligence. The intelligence about strategic...

*JH: Not accepted by Russia, by Germany, not accepted by France. You say accepted by everybody. Not by everybody.*

**TB:** Sorry, John. That isn't right. The resolution that was passed in the United Nations Security Council was a resolution that accepted that he was a weapons of mass destruction threat. The issue with France, Germany and Russia was that they thought there was a different way of dealing with it.

*JH: No, it wasn't that. 'Russia does not have in its possession any trustworthy data that would support the existence of nuclear weapons or any weapons of mass destruction in Iraq.' President Putin.*

**TB:** The weapons of mass destruction issue that was dealt with in resolution 1441, the whole of the international community accepted that this threat existed. That's why they called upon him to comply fully with the inspectors. Now let me go back to this issue...I think it's important. It's part of the...OK, in the end with this thing, I totally understand why people have a very strong view. You're entitled to have a view. Everyone's entitled to have a view. Just understand why I took this decision. I took the decision, as I said yesterday, I'm as fallible as anyone else. I may be wrong in it. But I don't believe I'm wrong.

*JH: If your judgement is wrong on this, if it really is wrong on this — let me put* this very bluntly – you wouldn't be fit to be Prime Minister, because you got wrong a profoundly important, the most important, decision...

**TB:** In the end, all you can do as Prime Minister is to say this is why I have taken this judgement. My judgement, post September 11, is that we face a completely new security threat. I really believe this. I believe it passionately. If we don't deal with this threat, then at some point in time, in the future, it is going to engulf us. There are different aspects of that. One aspect was dealing with regimes developing weapons of mass destruction that could fall into the hands of these terrorists. That is why we dealt with the issue of Iraq in UN resolutions. We could have dealt with it in a different way. We could have, for example, had Saddam complied. We could have dealt with that in a different way in respect of Iraq. We are dealing in a different way with Iran, with Libya, with North Korea.

**JH:** *Let me put this to you. What you did yesterday in your speech was set up two false opposites. You said there are two kinds of people, only two approaches. One approach is, say, we try not to provoke them. There are people who believe, just isolated individuals, extremists engaged in isolated acts of terrorism. They say 'Don't provoke them. Hope in time they will wither'. That is one group. I confess I haven't met that group, but you say there is that group. The other group, the other alternative — and there is no third way, you said — is to remove them, root and branch. But the point is there was, and is still, and there always is in these things, a third way. And in the case of Iraq, the third way was to carry on doing what we were doing, which was containment. What we've done instead, in your own words, is we have turned Iraq into a crucible of world terror. And you say the world is a safer place. Colin Powell himself tells us the world is not a safer place. There is more terrorism, not less.*

**TB:** Let's deal with this argument as well. You've been containing Saddam on and off for years. Why not just... It's an important argument. Why not say... It's important people hear from me why I don't think this argument is correct. I agree there was some success for the policy of containment in respect of weapons of mass destruction.

**JH:** *Total. There were no weapons of mass destruction.*

**TB:** The fact of the matter is we took bombing action actually at the end of 1998, and Robin Cook was Foreign Secretary... We had 2,000 British troops down there the whole time. No-fly-zones, sanctions, the question was...

**JH:** *And it was working.*

**TB:** Was it working?

**JH:** *Yes. We know it was because there were no weapons of mass destruction.*

**TB:** I don't know that we know that, actually.

*JH: I thought that was what you apologised for yesterday.*

**TB:** No. Because the issue is, was he prepared then to comply with UN resolutions? That's what I keep saying to you.

*JH: The issue is whether he was a threat to us.*

**TB:** And the question of whether he was a threat was whether he retained the capability and intent to develop weapons of mass destruction, I agree. Also, there's the issue of whether he had actual, readily deployable weapons. But the point that I'm making to you is, I don't accept that containment in respect of Saddam was working, and more than that, because I have taken this view that, after September 11, we've got to take a wholly different and more active approach to these issues, then containment of some sort or other is not sufficient to deal with this. We've got to go out and deal with it properly. As for the fact that Iraq is difficult today, of course it's difficult. But these are people who are there in Iraq trying to kill anybody, whether they're aid workers, Iraqi civilians, Iraqi people who want to join the police…

*JH: British soldiers.*

**TB:** Exactly, British soldiers. Why are they doing it? They're doing it… That's the question. That's why I say to you there are two views. What you say is, these people, if we hadn't given them the excuse, if we simply left them alone, there wouldn't be a problem. I don't agree with you. I profoundly disagree with you.

*JH: If it happens again, and this gets right down to the question of trust, and you've acknowledged that you have lost trust as a result of this. You said yesterday that the nation was divided over it, which clearly it is. If another situation like this arises, God forbid, and you have to go to the House of Commons and say 'There is this country that is threatening us, and it is developing weapons of mass destruction', isn't the truth that people would laugh at you. You simply couldn't do it.*

**TB:** It depends what the evidence is.

*JH: Does it? They'll say 'Hang on, we heard this before. And he had to tell us the intelligence was wrong, and he apologised'.*

**TB:** There's no point in hypothesizing.

*JH: This gets to the heart of the Prime Minister's responsibilities.*

**TB:** It does. I agree. But let's just get to the heart of it. I've taken this decision.

On the basis I'm not naïve about politics, it's a decision, let's say, in terms of popular support that has not done me a great deal of good. I think we'd both accept that. And sometimes when people talk about this issue of trust, the time to trust a politician most is actually when they're courting popularity least, because then they're doing something that, whatever the political price they're going to pay for it, they actually believe in. I keep saying to people I don't disrespect people who take another point of view. There is another point of view.

*JH: Let's not go down that road...*

**TB:** It's important in relation to the issue of trust. What it comes down to in the end is, am I doing this because I believe in it?...

*JH: No, it doesn't. What you believe in doesn't much matter, with great respect, in the sense that what matters is whether the people of this country would trust you to take them to war again. And if they would not trust you to take them to war again, you can't be Prime Minister, can you?*

**TB:** I'm afraid I don't accept that people won't trust a judgement that is made provided the evidence is given to them, and, of course, it's absolutely right the evidence given to them has got to be credible...

*JH: We had the evidence last time, and it was wrong.*

**TB:** There's no use in hypothesizing about what any future situation may bring. Of course, if it's a question of a country and weapons of mass destruction, never mind the rest of the country, I'm going to want to make sure that every single piece of evidence we assemble is right...

*JH: Didn't happen last time.*

**TB:** We did. The intelligence we got was very clear... and it was in respect of a country that had actually used weapons of mass destruction. It's not as if, when I went to the House in 2002, that we were talking about a country that had no history of weapons of mass destruction. We had inspectors in there with the wool pulled over their eyes...

*JH: Given what we know now, and what we knew then, you could actually see yourself standing in the House of Commons saying we have a dossier which proves x, y and z. The response to that would be, Prime Minister, people would be dismissive of you, wouldn't they?*

**TB:** We don't have such a situation. But the circumstances of it, of course, in the light of what has happened, people will want to know that any evidence that is given is very soundly based. But that's not the case at the moment, is it?

## Some questions still unresolved

Books have been written about the complex issues which have arisen from this terrible war. John Humphrys in the interview reproduced above deals with the issues admirably. But there are a few questions which deserve our commentary.

First, was the false information given out during the Prime Minister's advocacy of war 'given in good faith'? There is overwhelming evidence that it was not.[2] The latest and most comprehensive evidence from the United States comes from a Presidential Commission examining pre-war intelligence failures. A key source of this 'intelligence' was 'an alcoholic cousin of an aide to Ahmed Chalabi', who was held in contempt by his American handlers. They described him as 'crazy'. His own friends called him 'a congenital liar'. This defector is known by the code name Curveball, and Curveball is being held responsible for the comprehensive corruption of American intelligence estimates on Iraq.

> 'Of all the disproven pre-war weapons claims, from aluminium centrifuge tubes to yellowcake uranium from Niger, none points to greater levels of incompetence than those found within the misadventures of Curveball.'

None of the Americans had direct access to Curveball, whose reports came to them through German intelligence. But the Germans were profoundly suspicious of them. Between January 2000 and September 2001, Curveball submitted one hundred reports, including those on the claim of mobile biological weapons labs that were central to the claim of an illicit weapons programme, but turned out in fact to be trucks equipped with machinery to inflate weather balloons.

The Commission on the Intelligence Capabilities of the United States regarding Weapons of Mass Destruction reported that Curveball's information was worse than none at all. 'Worse than having no human sources' it said, 'is being seduced by a human source who is telling lies.'

Second, Tony Blair still insists that 'We took the action as a result of Saddam's failure to comply with UN resolutions'. What hard evidence is there for such non-compliance? Mr. Blair says that, 'In respect of regimes developing WMD, instead of taking a reactive approach, we had to take an active approach'. Britain itself has a large arsenal of weapons of mass destruction, including nuclear weapons. Who has appointed Britain, or for that matter, the United States, as custodian of world decisions on armaments?

Mr. Blair bases the legitimacy of this interventionism upon the attacks on Washington and New York on September 11th 2001. But Iraq had nothing whatever to do with these attacks. It is not even proven that the authorities in Afghanistan were associated with them. What is clear is that they were criminal attacks, and needed to be dealt with under the criminal law, which, if necessary, needed to be amended to be able to cover such events. If no States were involved in the attacks, then there was no legitimacy for counterattacks on States.

Since it is now beyond doubt that Iraq held no WMD stocks, the existence of 'a string of UN resolutions' takes on a different aspect, since many of them were clearly grounded on false intelligence. Be that as it may, it is untrue to say that the Iraqi regime did not comply in full with Resolution 1441 of the Security Council. The Iraqis submitted a 12,000 page Declaration in response to the demands of Resolution 1441, which has never been published, and has been withheld from all but the five Permanent Members of the Security Council.[3] But it was addressed to the Council as a whole, and there is no excuse for such censorship. Mr. Blair is therefore secure in the knowledge that the evidence on this matter is not available to a critical public.

Thirdly, Mr. Blair denies that the United Nations Secretary General is qualified to pronounce the war illegal. Specifically, he insists that, 'We believe if there was a breach of Resolution 1441 then we were justified in taking military action'. A long and noisy argument has skirted this issue, because it is assumed by many that this was the argument offered by the British Attorney General to justify war, at the end of a long process of equivocation. But the argument will not stand up for a moment. In fact, Resolution 1441 was accompanied by a formal statement by Ambassador Greenstock to the Security Council in an Explanation of Vote on the 8th November 2002:

> 'We heard loud and clear during the negotiation the concerns about "automaticity" and "hidden triggers" – the concern that on a decision so crucial we should not rush into military action; that on a decision so crucial any Iraqi violations should be discussed by the Council. Let me be equally clear in response, as a co-sponsor with the United States of the text we have adopted. There is no "automaticity" in this Resolution. If there is a further Iraqi breach of its disarmament obligations, the matter will return to the Council for discussion as required in Operational Paragraph 12. We would expect the Security Council then to meet its responsibilities.'

The Security Council did meet, of course, but the Resolution then favoured by Britain and the United States was withdrawn, since it was perfectly clear that if it went to the vote it would be thrown out. The new Resolution was not vetoed, because it was never tabled, and so there was no decision about what the responsibilities entailed might be.

This is the context in which Kofi Annan was later to insist that the decision to go to war by a tiny minority of Security Council members 'was not in conformity with the UN Charter…from the Charter point of view, it was illegal'.

Fourthly, Mr. Blair is still claiming that Iraq breached Resolution 1441. What breaches occurred? At the beginning of 2002, the Prime Minister insisted that Iraq had stockpiles 'of major amounts of chemical and biological weapons'. But the Joint Intelligence Committee in Britain was claiming that Iraq 'may have hidden small quantities of agents and weapons'. The Prime Minister claimed that 'Saddam Hussein poses a severe threat not just to the region, but to the wider world' and that he had sufficient chemical and biological weapons remaining to 'devastate the entire Gulf region'. But British intelligence estimated that 'Saddam has not succeeded in seriously threatening his neighbours'. These and other false allegations were accompanied by the claim that the Prime Minster had seen intelligence which was 'extensive, detailed and authoritative'. But the Chief of MI6 had in fact insisted to him that key sources should be treated with caution.

Every day brings new confessions by different parts of the intelligence community[4] about how their judgement on weapons of mass destruction has been at fault. If Tony Blair had not invested so much moral capital in buttressing these false claims, he might not deserve such strong criticism. Much of the untruth in the Government's case for war can be traced to the false information systematically fed to the Americans by Curveball. British intelligence apparently retailed this information: some treated it as if it were Gospel truth. Thus it became the Gospel according to Saint Tony, the most comprehensive farrago, in whose name have been slaughtered so many Iraqi children, and have been killed so many other innocents.

**Footnotes:**
1 We published a summary of this evidence in *The Spokesman*, in the number entitled *Falluja: Shock and Awe* (number 84, 2004).
2 See for instance: *www.impeachBlair.org A Case to Answer*, published by Spokesman Books, 2004.
3 A severely truncated version of the Declaration was circulated to the ten Non-Permanent Members of the Security Council. The censoring and suppression of Iraq's Declaration is recorded in *Empire No More!* (pages 187-199) by Ken Coates (Spokesman Books, 2004). See also *Dark Times: Torture* (The Spokesman no.81, 2004, pages 77-87).
4 Cf *The Times*, 8th April 2005: American chiefs admit Iraq's mistakes.

# II
## 'Intelligence and facts were being fixed around the policy'

*This highly revealing memorandum about the United Kingdom's position and preparations for war on Iraq, dating from July 2002, was leaked to the press in the days before the General Election. It speaks for itself and we reprint it in full.*

SECRET AND STRICTLY PERSONAL – UK EYES ONLY
To: DAVID MANNING
From: Matthew Rycroft
Date: 23 July 2002
S 195 /02
cc: Defence Secretary, Foreign Secretary, Attorney-General, Sir Richard Wilson, John Scarlett, Francis Richards, CDS [Chief of Defence Staff], C [Head of the Secret Intelligence Service], Jonathan Powell, Sally Morgan, Alastair Campbell

IRAQ: PRIME MINISTER'S MEETING, 23 JULY

Copy addressees and you met the Prime Minister on 23 July to discuss Iraq.
This record is extremely sensitive. No further copies should be made. It should be shown only to those with a genuine need to know its contents.

John Scarlett summarised the intelligence and latest Joint Intelligence Committee (JIC) assessment. Saddam's regime was tough and based on extreme fear. The only way to overthrow it was likely to be by massive military action. Saddam was worried and expected an attack, probably by air and land, but he was not convinced that it would be immediate or overwhelming. His regime expected their neighbours to line up with the US. Saddam knew that regular army morale was poor. Real support for Saddam among the public was probably narrowly based.

C reported on his recent talks in Washington. There was a perceptible shift in attitude. Military action was now seen as inevitable. Bush wanted to remove Saddam, through military action, justified by the conjunction of terrorism and weapons of mass destruction (WMD). But the intelligence and facts were being fixed around the policy. The National Security Council (NSC) had no patience with the UN route, and no enthusiasm for publishing material on the Iraqi regime's record. There was little discussion in Washington of the aftermath after military action.

The Chief of Defence Staff (CDS) said that military planners would brief US Central Command (CENTCOM) on 1-2 August, Rumsfeld on 3 August and Bush on 4 August.

The two broad US options were:
(a) Generated Start. A slow build-up of 250,000 US troops, a short (72 hour) air campaign, then a move up to Baghdad from the south. Lead time of 90 days (30 days preparation plus 60 days deployment to Kuwait).
(b) Running Start. Use forces already in theatre (3 x 6,000), continuous air campaign, initiated by an Iraqi *casus belli*. Total lead time of 60 days with the air campaign beginning even earlier. A hazardous option.

The US saw the UK (and Kuwait) as essential, with basing in Diego Garcia and Cyprus critical for either option. Turkey and other Gulf states were also important, but less vital. The three main options for UK involvement were:
(i) Basing in Diego Garcia and Cyprus, plus three Special Forces (SF) squadrons.
(ii) As above, with maritime and air assets in addition.
(iii) As above, plus a land contribution of up to 40,000, perhaps with a discrete role in Northern Iraq entering from Turkey, tying down two Iraqi divisions.

The Defence Secretary said that the US had already begun 'spikes of activity' to put pressure on the regime. No decisions had been taken, but he thought the most likely timing in US minds for military action to begin was January, with the timeline beginning 30 days before the US Congressional elections.

The Foreign Secretary said he would discuss this with Colin Powell this week. It seemed clear that Bush had made up his mind to take military action, even if the timing was not yet decided. But the case was thin. Saddam was not threatening his neighbours, and his WMD capability was less than that of Libya, North Korea or Iran. We should work up a plan for an ultimatum to Saddam to allow back in the UN weapons inspectors. This would also help with the legal justification for the use of force.

The Attorney-General said that the desire for regime change was not a legal base for military action. There were three possible legal bases: self-defence, humanitarian intervention, or United Nations Security Council (UNSC) authorisation. The first and second could not be the base in this case. Relying on UNSCR 1205 of three years ago would be difficult. The situation might of course change.

The Prime Minister said that it would make a big difference politically and legally if Saddam refused to allow in the UN inspectors. Regime change and weapons of mass destruction were linked in the sense that it was the regime that was producing the weapons of mass destruction. There were different strategies for dealing with Libya and Iran. If the political context were right, people would support regime change. The two key issues were whether the military plan worked and whether we had the political strategy to give the military plan the space to work.

On the first, the Chief of Defence Staff said that we did not know yet if the US battleplan was workable. The military were continuing to ask lots of questions.

For instance, what were the consequences, if Saddam used weapons of mass destruction on day one, or if Baghdad did not collapse and urban warfighting began? You said that Saddam could also use his weapons of mass destruction on Kuwait. Or on Israel, added the Defence Secretary.

The Foreign Secretary thought the US would not go ahead with a military plan unless convinced that it was a winning strategy. On this, US and UK interests converged. But on the political strategy, there could be US/UK differences. Despite US resistance, we should explore discreetly the ultimatum. Saddam would continue to play hard-ball with the UN.

John Scarlett assessed that Saddam would allow the inspectors back in only when he thought the threat of military action was real.

The Defence Secretary said that if the Prime Minister wanted UK military involvement, he would need to decide this early. He cautioned that many in the US did not think it worth going down the ultimatum route. It would be important for the Prime Minister to set out the political context to Bush.

Conclusions:
(a) We should work on the assumption that the UK would take part in any military action. But we needed a fuller picture of US planning before we could take any firm decisions. The Chief of Defence Staff should tell the US military that we were considering a range of options.
(b) The Prime Minister would revert on the question of whether funds could be spent in preparation for this operation.
(c) The Chief of Defence Staff would send the Prime Minister full details of the proposed military campaign and possible UK contributions by the end of the week.
(d) The Foreign Secretary would send the Prime Minister the background on the UN inspectors, and discreetly work up the ultimatum to Saddam. He would also send the Prime Minister advice on the positions of countries in the region especially Turkey, and of the key EU member states.
(e) John Scarlett would send the Prime Minister a full intelligence update.
(f) We must not ignore the legal issues: the Attorney-General would consider legal advice with Foreign and Commonwealth Office/Ministry of Defence legal advisers.

(I have written separately to commission this follow-up work.)
MATTHEW RYCROFT
(Rycroft was a Downing Street foreign policy aide)

## III
## Sedgefield contested

*Tony Blair represents the former mining constituency of Sedgefield in the British Parliament. In the 2005 Election, he was opposed by Reg Keys, a paramedic whose son was killed in Iraq in June 2003. This protest candidature drew support from all over the country, and when the result was declared, Mr Blair finally had to listen to his opponent explain why he had stood against him. This is what Reg Keys said:*

'Fighting this campaign has not been an easy task for me, but I had to do it for my son, Thomas Keys, Royal Military Policeman, killed in Iraq four days short of his 21$^{st}$ birthday. He was sent to war under extremely controversial circumstances...(*turning to Mr Blair*) extremely controversial circumstances.

If this war had been justified by international law, I would have grieved and not campaigned. If weapons of mass destruction had been found in Iraq, I would have grieved and not campaigned.

Tonight there are lessons to be learned, and I hope in my heart that one day the Prime Minister will be able to say sorry, that one day he will say sorry to the families of the bereaved, and that one day the Prime Minister might be able to visit wounded soldiers in hospital.

Then our campaign will not have been in vain, and all the people who have given me their votes tonight have sent a clear resounding message about the Iraq war.

I would like to dedicate this campaign to all the brave 88, yes 88, British servicemen – because some people do not know how many have been killed *(a reference to Mr Blair's admission on radio that he did not know the exact figure)* – servicemen who gave their young lives in this conflict.

But may I just in particular mention, as they have become known, The Six, the six Royal Military Policemen left behind and slaughtered in a filthy police station in Al Majar Al-Kabir: Thomas Keys, Russell Aston, Simon Miller, Paul Long, Benjamin Hyde and Simon Hamilton-Jewell. '

*For more information see http://www.keysforsedgefield.org.uk/*

## IV
## Military families serve notice on Blair

*On 3 May 2005, Rose and Maxine Gentle, Peter and Helen Brierley, and Tony Hamilton-Jewell delivered to Downing Street this letter from their lawyers demanding an independent Public Inquiry into the war on Iraq in which their relatives died.*

Dear Mr Blair

We act for Reg and Sally Keys, Rose and George Gentle, Teresa and Tony Hamilton-Jewell, Anna Aston and Peter Brierley, John and Marilyn Miller, George and Ann Lawrence, Tracey Pritchard, Patricia Long and Sharon Hehir. Our clients are the relatives of serving members of the UK Armed Forces who gave their lives during the Iraq War and the subsequent occupation.

*Our Clients*

Reg and Sally Keys are the parents of Lance Corporal Thomas Keys, who was killed in Al Majar Al-Kabir, near Basra, Southern Iraq on 24 June 2003 while serving with 156 Provost Company, Royal Military Police.

Teresa Hamilton-Jewell is the mother and Tony Hamilton-Jewell is the brother of Sergeant Simon Hamilton-Jewell, who was killed in Al Majar Al-Kabir, near Basra, Southern Iraq on 24 June 2003 while serving with 156 Provost Company, Royal Military Police.

John and Marilyn Miller are the parents of Corporal Simon Miller, who was killed in Al Majar Al-Kabir, near Basra, Southern Iraq on 24 June 2003 while serving with 156 Provost Company, Royal Military Police.

Anna Aston is the wife of Corporal Russell Aston, who was killed in Al Majar Al-Kabir, near Basra, Southern Iraq on 24 June 2003 while serving with 156 Provost Company, Royal Military Police.

Peter Brierley is the father of Lance Corporal Shaun Brierley, who was killed in a road traffic accident in Kuwait on 30 March 2003 while serving with 1st (UK) Armoured Division Headquarters and Signal Regiment.

Rose and George Gentle are the parents of Fusilier Gordon Gentle, who was killed in an improvised explosive device attack on British military vehicles on 28 June 2004 while serving with 1st Battalion Royal Highland Fusiliers.

George and Ann Lawrence are the parents of Lieutenant Marc Lawrence, who was killed at sea when two Royal Navy helicopters collided on 22 March 2003 while serving with the Royal Navy.

Tracey Pritchard is the wife of Corporal Dewi Pritchard, who was killed in a gun attack on 23 August while serving with the Territorial Army.

Patricia Long is the mother of Corporal Paul Long, who was killed in Al Majar Al-Kabir, near Basra, Southern Iraq on 24 June 2003 while serving with 156 Provost Company, Royal Military Police.

Sharon Hehir is the wife of Sergeant Les Hehir, who was killed in a US helicopter crash on March 21 2003 while serving with the Royal Artillery.

*The Demand*

Our clients are demanding that you direct that a fully independent Public Inquiry is set up into the deaths of their loved ones, that thoroughly investigates the legality of the war against Iraq, and examines whether you and your government misled their loved ones and themselves about the basis on which the United Kingdom entered Iraq, an action which led to the loss of the lives of their relatives.

*The Factual Basis for the Demand*

Each one of our clients' loved ones was a brave and courageous individual who joined the British Army in order to serve his country. They all knew that as soldiers they would be asked to place their lives in peril and did so understanding that their leaders would only ask them to act in circumstances that were in the national interest and were lawful. Each of our clients' loved ones was killed at a time when they had been told by you that they were fighting a war that was fully justified in international law in order to disarm a country that held weapons of mass destruction ('WMD') which threatened international peace and security.

It has long been apparent that the stated rationale for the war, namely the presence of weapons of mass destruction, was incorrect in that no such weapons existed either at the date at which our clients' loved ones were sent to Iraq nor at the date of their deaths. In the past days our clients have witnessed with anger the disclosure of documentation that throws into grave doubt the supposed justification and rationale for the war, and moreover could be said to raise reasonable doubt on whether you ordered their loved ones into battle in good faith. They have read papers which seem to suggest:

(a) That on March 14th 2002 (through your Foreign Policy Adviser Sir David Manning) you told Condoleezza Rice that you '*would not budge in your support for regime change, but you had to manage a press, a parliament and a public opinion*';

(b) That in April 2002 during the course of a meeting with President Bush you again agreed that the UK would support military action to bring about regime change in Iraq;

(c) That in a meeting on the 23rd July 2002 the Attorney General advised you in clear and categoric terms that regime change was not a legal basis for military action;

(d) That at that meeting on the 23rd July 2002 the Foreign Secretary advised you that the case for war was 'thin' in that Saddam was not threatening his neighbours and his WMD capability was less that that of Libya, North Korea or Iran;

(e) The Foreign Secretary advised you to work up a plan to issue an ultimatum to Saddam to allow back UN weapons inspectors in part to help with the legal justification for war;

(f) The Attorney General further advised you at that July 2002 meeting that legal arguments which sought to place reliance upon previous resolutions of the Security Council would be difficult;

(g) In an Advice dated 7th March 2003 the Attorney General repeated his opinion that it would be unlawful to base military action on regime change;

(h) He further noted that the legal arguments that placed reliance on previous Security Council resolutions were 'reasonably arguable' but that a Court 'might well' conclude otherwise. This was despite his opinion in the previous July that such arguments were 'difficult' and his undertaking then to liaise with Foreign and Commomwealth Office and Ministry of Defence legal advisers;

(i) That in order for such a legal argument to be 'sustainable' there would have to be 'strong factual grounds' and 'hard evidence' of Iraqi non-compliance and that in this regard the views of UNMOVIC and the International Atomic Energy Agency would be 'highly significant'.

These matters disclosed in recent days stand in stark contrast to the repeated declarations that you have made as to the basis for war and also seem very difficult to reconcile with the unequivocal terms of the Attorney General's published summary of his Advice of 17 March 2003.

In the light of the disparity between the unofficially disclosed documents and official public pronouncements our clients have a number of very real concerns as to the legality and legitimacy of the basis on which their loved ones sacrificed their lives. For example:

(1) At the very least, a reasonable suspicion arises that you committed the UK (and thus our clients' loved ones) to war on the basis of regime change;
(2) You did so knowing that this was an unlawful basis for war and having been advised so in explicit terms by the Attorney General;
(3) You developed a political strategy of focusing on weapons of mass destruction and the return of the UN Inspectors for the improper purpose of seeking justification for the improper motive of effecting regime change in Iraq;
(4) You failed to direct the military to conduct their strategy exclusively on considerations of military objectives and necessity that were proportionate to disarmament rather than regime change;
(5) That when asked by the Attorney General on 14 March 2003 for an assurance that it was 'unequivocally [your view] that Iraq has committed further material breaches as specified in paragraph 4 of resolution 1441' you gave that assurance on 15 March. Our clients submit that given the state of the intelligence, and the understanding of UNMOVIC as to the existence of weapons of mass destruction, at that time, you had no proper or lawful basis for such an 'unequivocal view'.

Our clients are also extremely concerned as to the changing nature of the Attorney General's advice and separately as to the use to which it was made, in particular:

(1) The Attorney General's initial view was that it would be difficult to rely on previous United Nations Security Council resolutions to provide a legal justification for military action. We understand that subsequent to this he received advice from the Foreign and Commonwealth Office legal advisers that such an argument would not succeed and that the proposed military action would be unlawful. This view mirrors that of effectively the entire community of independent international law practitioners and academics;
(2) Notwithstanding the above by March 7 2003 the Attorney General held that the revival argument was arguable and that it was reasonably arguable that it would apply to SC 1441 albeit that a Court might well conclude otherwise;
(3) Within the space of 10 days his opinion on this discrete point of law appeared to change from a guarded, qualified expression of 'arguability' to a unequivocal declaration of legality;
(4) There is no evidence to suggest that 'highly significant' views of UNMOVIC were sought and indeed it is most unlikely that they were, for as Mr Blix has repeatedly asserted, he would have gainsaid suggestions of hard evidence of non-compliance;
(5) In light of what is now known about the presence of weapons of mass destruction in Iraq it is very difficult for our clients to understand what 'hard

evidence' you could have properly presented to the Attorney General in order for him to conclude that war would be lawful.

All the matters set out above bear directly upon the question as to whether there was a lawful basis to send our clients' loved ones to Iraq. What emerges from the documentation is a reasonable suspicion that they were sent to their deaths for an unlawful purpose, namely regime change for the sake of regime change, carried out simply to support a US foreign policy aim which had never been (nor could it ever in itself lawfully be) a policy of this country.

## *The Legal Basis for the Demand*

As you know, Article 2 of the European Convention on Human Rights imposes an obligation on you and your government to protect the lives of those under your authority and control. Clearly members of the armed services voluntarily expose themselves to a greater degree of risk than most but nevertheless the obligation rests on the State under Article 2 to take steps to protect them from unnecessary risks. The material decisions leading up to the deaths of our clients' loved ones were all taken whilst they were within the jurisdictional reach of the European Convention on Human Rights even if our clients were on overseas basis at any material time (see *Al-Skeini v SSD* [2004] EWHC 2911 para 245). If it were established that you sent our clients' loved ones to war on an unlawful basis, knowing that in so doing you were exposing them to a quite unnecessary risk of death, then that would have plainly infringed their Article 2 rights.

As you will also be aware whenever a death occurs in circumstances in which the role of the State might be suspicious an obligation arises to conduct a thorough and independent investigation into the cause of death. This is a requirement recognised not only by the Strasbourg Court (see for example *Edwards v United Kingdom* 35 WHHR 487 and *Jordan v United Kingdom* 37 EHRR 52) but recently underlined by the House of Lords in *R v Amin* [2004] 1 AC 653 as now being part of our domestic law. We would say that, in any event, basic standards of accountability at public law would call for such an inquiry.

Accordingly, our clients demand a full public independent Inquiry.

Only such a forum, that can enable our clients to learn the full circumstances surrounding the decision to send their loved ones to war, will meet the imperative for the government to be both held to account and put in a position where it has to take steps to ensure that such a breach does not occur again.

## *The Nature of the Inquiry Demanded*

As Lord Bingham noted in *Amin* (para 31) the purpose of an Article 2 compliant inquiry is clear: to ensure that so far as possible the full facts are brought to light; that culpable and discreditable conduct is exposed and brought to public notice; that suspicion of deliberate wrongdoing if unjustified is allayed; that dangerous practices and procedures are rectified, and that those who have lost their relatives may at least have the satisfaction of knowing that lessons learned from the deaths may save future lives.

Any such Inquiry will have to comply with the basic pre-requisites for any investigation into deaths in circumstances as serious as this, namely:
(1) It will have to be independent;
(2) It will have to be effective in that it is capable of leading to a determination of the basis on which the UK actually went to war;
(3) It will need to be held in public – in a case of this importance this is the only means of securing public scrutiny;
(4) It will have to allow for meaningful participation from the family including representation by lawyers who are permitted to question witnesses;
(5) In a case of this importance it is indispensable that proper procedures must allow for the mandatory surrender of all relevant documentation and attendance of witnesses.

As you know, the basis on which we went to war is a matter of the utmost public concern as well as being a deeply personal matter for our clients. Neither our clients nor the public will be satisfied with anything less than the most transparently independent and thorough investigation. In the circumstances they would request that the government makes it plain that the Inquiry should be outwith the restrictive scope of the Inquiries Act 2005.

We await your response within 14 days of today's date.

Yours faithfully

*Public Interest Lawyers*

# 'Curveball'
## Feeding False Intelligence

Charles S Robb
&
Laurence H Silberman

*Tony Simpson selected and edited these excerpts from the Report of The Commission on the Intelligence Capabilities of the United States Regarding Weapons of Mass Destruction, chaired by Mr Robb and Judge Silberman.*

*The Commission on the Intelligence Capabilities of the United States Regarding Weapons of Mass Destruction submitted its Report to President Bush on 31 March 2005. Iraq was one among several case studies examined by the Commission. It threw some light on how Colin Powell came to present completely false information about alleged Iraqi biological weapons to the United Nations Security Council, in February 2003, as he and Jack Straw tried unsuccessfully to garner support for war on Iraq. Mr Powell's source was known as 'Curveball', and was described as 'crazy' by his German handlers. We reprint part of this case study below, and follow it with some remarks about the manipulations of intelligence services in pursuit of making the case for war on Iraq, which appear on Al Jazeera.com's web site section entitled 'Conspiracy Theories'.*

...When information from Curveball first surfaced in early 2000, [Department of] Defense Human Intelligence did nothing to validate Curveball's reporting. Analysts within the Intelligence Community, however, did make efforts to assess the credibility of the information provided by Curveball. In early 2000, when Curveball's reporting first surfaced, Weapons Intelligence, Nonproliferation and Arms Control Center (CIA) analysts researched previous reporting and concluded that Curveball's information was plausible based upon previous intelligence, including imagery reporting, and the detailed, technical descriptions of the mobile facilities he provided. As a Weapons Intelligence, Nonproliferation and Arms Control Center biological weapons analyst later told us, there was nothing 'obviously wrong' with Curveball's information, and his story – that Iraq had moved to a mobile capability for its biological weapons programme in 1995 in order to evade inspectors – was logical in light of other known information.

> **Commission Finding**
> 
> Indications of possible problems with Curveball began to emerge well before the 2002 National Intelligence Estimate. These early indications of problems – which suggested unstable behaviour more than a lack of credibility – were discounted by the analysts working the Iraq weapons of mass destruction account. But given these warning signs, analysts should have viewed Curveball's information with greater scepticism and should have conveyed this scepticism in the National Intelligence Estimate. The analysts' resistance to any information that could undermine Curveball's reliability suggests that the analysts were unduly wedded to a source that supported their assumptions about Iraq's biological weapons programmes.

At about the same time, however, traffic in the CIA's Directorate of Operations began to suggest some possible problems with Curveball. The first CIA concerns about Curveball's reliability arose within the Directorate of Operations in May 2000, when a Department of Defense detailee assigned to the Directorate met Curveball. The purpose of the meeting was to evaluate Curveball's claim that he had been present during a biological weapons accident that killed several of his co-workers by seeing whether Curveball had been exposed to, or vaccinated against, a biological weapons agent. Although the evaluation was ultimately inconclusive, the detailee raised several concerns about Curveball based on their interaction.

First, the detailee observed that Curveball spoke excellent English during their meeting. This was significant to the detailee because the foreign service had, on several earlier occasions, told United States intelligence officials that one reason a meeting with Curveball was impossible was that Curveball did not speak English. Second, the detailee was concerned by Curveball's apparent 'hangover' during their meeting. The detailee conveyed these impressions of Curveball informally to CIA officials, and Weapons Intelligence, Non-proliferation and Arms Control Center biological weapons analysts told Commission staff that they were aware that the detailee was concerned that Curveball might be an alcoholic. This message was eventually re-conveyed to Directorate of Operations supervisors via electronic mail on February 4, 2003 – literally on the eve of Secretary Powell's speech to the United Nations. The electronic mail stated, in part:

> 'I do have a concern with the validity of the information based on Curveball having a terrible hangover the morning of [the meeting]. I agree, it was only a one time interaction, however, he knew he was to have a [meeting] on that particular morning but tied one on anyway. What underlying issues could this be a problem with and how in depth has he been vetted by the [foreign liaison service]?'

By early 2001, the Directorate of Operations was receiving operational messages about the foreign service's difficulties in handling Curveball, whom the foreign service reported to be 'out of control,' and whom the service could not locate. This operational traffic regarding Curveball was shared with the Weapons Intelligence,

Non-proliferation and Arms Control Center's Iraq biological weapons analysts because, according to the Center's analysts, the primary biological weapons analyst who worked on the Iraq issue had close relations with the Directorate's Counter-proliferation Division (the division through which the operational traffic was primarily handled). This and other operational information was not, however, shared with analysts outside the Central Intelligence Agency.

A second warning on Curveball came in April 2002, when a foreign intelligence service, which was also receiving reporting from Curveball, told the CIA that, in its view, there were a variety of problems with Curveball. The foreign service began by noting that they were 'inclined to believe that a significant part of [Curveball's] reporting is true' in light of his detailed technical descriptions. In this same message, however, the foreign service noted that it was 'not convinced that Curveball is a wholly reliable source,' and that 'elements of [Curveball's] behaviour strike us as typical of individuals we would normally assess as fabricators.' Even more specifically, the foreign service noted several inconsistencies in Curveball's reporting which caused the foreign service 'to have doubts about Curveball's reliability.' It should be noted here that, like the handling foreign service, this other service continued officially to back Curveball's reporting throughout this period.

Again, these concerns about Curveball were shared with CIA analysts working on the biological weapons issue. But none of the expressed concerns overcame analysts' ultimate confidence in the accuracy of his information. Specifically, analysts continued to judge his information credible based on their assessment of its detail and technical accuracy, corroborating documents, confirmation of the technical feasibility of the production facility designs described by Curveball, and reporting from another human source .... But it should be noted that during the pre-National Intelligence Estimate period – in addition to the more general questions about Curveball's credibility discussed above – at least some evidence had emerged calling into question the substance of Curveball's reporting about Iraq's biological weapons programme as well.

Specifically, a Weapons Intelligence, Non-proliferation and Arms Control Center biological weapons analyst told us that two foreign services had both noted in 2001 that Curveball's description of the facility he claimed was involved in the mobile biological weapons programme was contradicted by imagery of the site, which showed a wall across the path that Curveball said the mobile trailers traversed. Intelligence Community analysts 'set that information aside,' however, because it could not be reconciled with the rest of Curveball's information, which appeared plausible. Analysts also explained away this discrepancy by noting that Iraq had historically been very successful in 'denial and deception' activities and speculated that the wall spotted by imagery might be a temporary structure put up by the Iraqis to deceive United States intelligence efforts.

Analysts' use of denial and deception to explain away discordant evidence about Iraq's biological weapons programmes was a recurring theme in our review of the Community's performance on the biological weapons question. Burned by the experience of being wrong on Iraq's weapons of mass destruction in 1991 and convinced that Iraq was restarting its programmes, analysts dismissed indications that Iraq had actually abandoned its prohibited programmes by chalking these indicators up to Iraq's well-known denial and deception efforts. In one instance, for example, Weapons Intelligence, Non-proliferation and Arms Control Center analysts described reporting from the second source indicating Iraq was filling biological weapons warheads at a transportable facility near Baghdad. When imagery was unable to locate the transportable biological weapons systems at the reported site, analysts assumed this was not because the activity was not taking place, but rather because Iraq was hiding activities from US satellite overflights. This tendency was best encapsulated by a comment in a memorandum prepared by the Central Intelligence Agency for a senior policymaker: 'Mobile biological weapons information comes from [several] sources, one of whom is credible and the other is of undetermined reliability. We have raised our collection posture in a bid to locate these production units, but years of fruitless searches by the United Nations Special Commission (UNSCOM) indicate they are well hidden.' Again, the analysts appear never to have considered the idea that the searches were fruitless because the weapons were not there.

---

***Commission Finding***
The October 2002 National Intelligence Estimate failed to communicate adequately to policymakers both the Community's near-total reliance on Curveball for its biological weapons judgments, and the serious problems that characterized Curveball as a source.

---

The Community erred in failing to highlight its overwhelming reliance on Curveball for its biological weapons assessments. The National Intelligence Estimate judged that Iraq 'has transportable facilities for producing bacterial and toxin biological weapons agents' and attributed this judgment to multiple sources. In reality, however, on the topic of mobile biological weapons facilities Curveball provided approximately 100 detailed reports on the subject, while the second and fourth sources each provided a single report ... The presentation of the material as attributable to 'multiple sensitive sources,' however, gave the impression that the support for the biological weapons assessments was more broadly based than was in fact the case. A more accurate presentation would have allowed senior officials to see just how narrow the evidentiary base for the judgments on Iraq's biological weapons programmes actually was.

Other contemporaneous assessments about Iraq's biological weapons programme also reflect this problem. For example, the Intelligence Community informed senior policymakers in July 2002 that CIA judged that 'Baghdad has transportable production facilities for biological weapons agents...according to defectors.' Again, while three 'defector' sources (Curveball, the second source, and the Iraqi National Congress source) are cited in this report, Curveball's reporting was the overwhelmingly predominant source of the information.

And the National Intelligence Estimate should not only have emphasised its reliance on Curveball for its biological weapons judgments; it should also have communicated the limitations of the source himself. The National Intelligence Estimate, for instance, described him as 'an Iraqi defector deemed credible by the [Intelligence Community].' The use of the term 'credible' was apparently meant to imply only that Curveball's reporting was technically plausible. To a lay reader, however, it implied a broader judgment as to the source's general reliability. This description obscured a number of salient facts that, given the Community's heavy reliance upon his reporting, would have been highly important for policymakers to know – including the fact that the Community had never gained direct access to the source and that he was known at the time to have serious handling problems. While policymakers may still have credited his reporting, they would at least have been warned about the risks in doing so.

> ***Commission Finding***
> Beginning in late 2002, some operations officers within the regional division of the CIA's Directorate of Operations that was responsible for relations with the liaison service handling Curveball expressed serious concerns about Curveball's reliability to senior officials at the CIA, but these views were either (1) not thought to outweigh analytic assessments that Curveball's information was reliable or (2) disregarded because of managers' assessments that those views were not sufficiently convincing to warrant further elevation.

After the National Intelligence Estimate was published, but before Secretary Powell's speech to the United Nations, more serious concerns surfaced about Curveball's reliability. These concerns were never brought to Secretary Powell's attention, however. Precisely how and why this lapse occurred is the subject of dispute and conflicting memories. This section provides only a brief summary of the key events in this complicated saga.

The National Intelligence Estimate went to press in early October 2002, but its publication did not end the need to scrutinise Curveball's reliability. To improve the CIA's confidence in Curveball, the CIA's Deputy Director for Operations (DDO), James Pavitt, sought to press the foreign intelligence service for access to Curveball. Mr. Pavitt's office accordingly asked the chief ('the division chief') of the Directorate of Operation's regional division responsible for relations with the liaison service ('the division') to meet with a representative of the foreign intelligence service to make the request for access. According to the division chief, he met with the representative in late September or early October 2002.

At the lunch, the division chief raised the issue of US intelligence officials speaking to Curveball directly. According to the division chief, the representative of the foreign intelligence service responded with words to the effect of 'You don't want to see him [Curveball] because he's crazy.' Speaking to him would be, in the representative of the foreign service's words, 'a waste of time.' The representative, who said that he had been present for debriefings of Curveball, continued that his intelligence service was not sure whether Curveball was actually telling the truth and, in addition, that he had serious doubts about Curveball's mental stability and reliability; Curveball, according to the representative, had had a nervous breakdown. Further, the representative said that he worried that Curveball was 'a fabricator.' The representative cautioned the division chief, however, that the foreign service would publicly and officially deny these views if pressed. The representative told the division chief that the rationale for such a public denial would be that the foreign service did not wish to be embarrassed. According to the division chief, he passed the information to three offices: up the line to the office of CIA's Deputy Director for Operations; down the line to his staff, specifically the division's group chief ('the group chief') responsible for the liaison country's region; and across the agency to the Weapons Intelligence, Non-proliferation and Arms Control Center. At the time, the division chief thought that the information was 'no big deal' because he did not realise how critical Curveball's reporting was to the overall case for Iraqi possession of a biological weapons programme. He assumed there were other streams of reporting to buttress the Intelligence Community's assessments. He could not imagine, he said, that Curveball was 'it.'

Several months later, prompted by indications that the President or a senior US official would soon be making a speech on Iraq's weapons of mass destruction programmes, one of the executive assistants for the then-Deputy Director of Central Intelligence (DDCI) John McLaughlin met with the group chief to look into the Curveball information. This meeting took place on December 18, 2002. Although the executive assistant did not specifically recall the meeting when he spoke with Commission staff, an electronic mail follow-up from the meeting – which was sent to the division chief and the group chief – makes clear that the meeting was called to discuss Curveball and the public use of his information.

As a result of this meeting, the division sent a message that same afternoon to the CIA's station in the relevant country again asking that the foreign intelligence service permit the United States to debrief Curveball. The message stressed the importance of gaining access to Curveball, and noted the US government's desire to use Curveball's reporting publicly. On December 20, the foreign service refused the request for access, but concurred with the request to use Curveball's information publicly – 'with the expectation of source protection.'

By this point, it was clear that the division believed there was a serious problem with Curveball that required attention. A second meeting was scheduled on December 19 at the invitation of DDCI McLaughlin's same executive assistant. According to the executive assistant, he called the meeting because it had become apparent to Deputy Director of Central Intelligence McLaughlin that Curveball's reporting was significant to the Intelligence Community's judgments on Iraq's mobile biological weapons capability. The invitation for the meeting stated that the purpose was to 'resolve precisely how we judge Curveball's reporting on mobile biological weapons labs,' and that the executive assistant hoped that after the meeting he could 'summarise [the] conclusions in a short note to the Deputy

Director of Central Intelligence.' The meeting was attended by the executive assistant, a Weapons Intelligence, Non-proliferation and Arms Control Center biological weapons analyst, an operations officer from the Directorate of Operations's Counter-proliferation Division, and the regional division's group chief. Mr. McLaughlin, who did not attend this meeting, told this Commission that he was not given a written summary of the meeting and did not recall whether any such meeting was held.

Although individuals' recollections of the meeting vary somewhat, there is little disagreement on the meeting's substance. The group chief argued that Curveball had not been adequately 'vetted' and that his information should therefore not be relied upon. In preparation for the meeting, the group chief had outlined her concerns in an electronic mail to several officers within the Directorate of Operations – including Stephen Kappes, the then-Associate Deputy Director for Operations. The electronic mail opened with the following (in bold type):

> 'Although no one asked, it is my assessment that Curve Ball had some access to some of this information and was more forthcoming and cooperative when he needed resettlement assistance; now that he does not need it, he is less helpful, possibly because when he was being helpful, he was embellishing, a bit. The [foreign service] ha[s] developed some doubts about him. We have been unable to vet him operationally and know very little about him. The intelligence community has corroborated portions of his reporting with open source information ... and some intelligence (which appears to confirm that things are where he said they were).'

At the meeting, the group chief stated that she told the attendees that the division's concerns were based on the foreign service representative's statements to the division chief, the CIA's inability to get access to Curveball, the significant 'improvement' in Curveball's reporting over time, the decline of Curveball's reporting after he received the equivalent of a green card, among other reasons. She also recalled telling the attendees the details of the foreign service representative's statements to the division chief. In the group chief's view, she made it clear to all the attendees that the division did not believe that Curveball's information should be relied upon.

With equal vigour, the Weapons Intelligence, Non-proliferation and Arms Control Center representative argued that Curveball's reporting was fundamentally reliable. According to the Center analyst, Curveball's information was reliable because it was detailed, technically accurate, and corroborated by another source's reporting.

Both the group chief and the Center analyst characterised the exchange as fairly heated. Both of the two primary participants also recalled providing reasons why the other's arguments should not carry the day. Specifically, the group chief says she argued, adamantly, that the supposedly corroborating information was of dubious significance because it merely established that Curveball had been to the location, not that he had any knowledge of biological weapons activities being conducted there. In addition, the group chief questioned whether some of

Curveball's knowledge could have come from readily available, open source materials. Conversely, the Weapons Intelligence, Non-proliferation and Arms Control Center biological weapons analyst says that she questioned whether the group chief had sufficient knowledge of Curveball's reporting to be able to make an accurate assessment of his reliability.

It appears that the Weapons Intelligence, Non-proliferation and Arms Control Center prevailed in this argument. Looking back, the executive assistant who had called the meeting offered his view that the Center Biological Weapons analyst was the 'master of [the Curveball] case,' and that he 'look[ed] to her for answers.' He also noted that the group chief clearly expressed her scepticism about Curveball during the meeting, and that she fundamentally took the position that Curveball's reporting did not 'hold up.' The executive assistant further said that while the foreign service officially assessed that Curveball was reliable, they also described him as a 'handling problem.' According to the executive assistant, the foreign service said Curveball was a handling problem because he was a drinker, unstable, and generally difficult to manage. In the executive assistant's view, however, it was impossible to know whether the foreign service's description of Curveball was accurate. Finally, the executive assistant said that he fully recognised Curveball's significance at the time of the meeting; that Curveball 'was clearly the most significant source' on biological weapons; and that if Curveball were removed, the biological weapons assessment was left with one other human source, 'but not much more'…

\* \* \*

## Fomenting war by manipulating intelligence

In an interview with Vincent Cannistaro, the former CIA head of counterterrorism operations and intelligence director at the National Security Council under Ronald Reagan, Mr Cannistaro was asked if the documents on Iraq's purchase of uranium from Niger came from Italian intelligence, to which he answered in the affirmative.

However, according to Cannistaro '…When we're talking about acquiring information on Iraq, it isn't that anyone had a good source on Iraq – there weren't any good sources. The Italian intelligence service, the military intelligence service, was acquiring information that was really being hand-fed to them by very dubious sources. The Niger documents, for example, which apparently were produced in the United States, yet were funnelled through the Italians.'

When the former CIA head of counter-terrorism was asked if a Michael Ledeen had been the one who produced the Iraq documents he said 'You'd be very close.' This is consistent with the theory that the documents are the work of Iraqi dissidents associated with Ahmed Chalabi's Iraqi National Congress. The documents would have flowed from Chalabi to Ledeen to Italian intelligence, and thus would have been laundered to make them appear as legitimate products discovered by a legitimate intelligence agency.

This sophistication in the use of foreign intelligence agencies appears to be part of the *modus operandi* of the neocons, and may perhaps derive from the particular expertise of Ledeen and Richard Perle, developed in various shenanigans going back to the 1970s, in particular the Iran-Contra affair.

Intelligence agencies in Britain, France, and Germany were also used in the same campaigns of lies which led to the attack on Iraq. One of the strategies was to feed some nonsense to one intelligence agency, and then have that nonsense distributed to other intelligence agencies. Then the claim would be that the information must be true, as it came from multiple sources.

The handling of the source of the main lies used to justify the attack, the aptly named 'Curveball', also displays the same sophistication in technique. Curveball was too obviously undependable to be sent directly to the CIA. As Joseph Cannon writes:

> '...the [Office of Special Plans] could feed lies directly into the Oval Office – but they needed more. They needed to find a way to make the CIA bestow its imprimatur onto this silliness. Thus, the neocons somehow arranged for Curveball to be routed through German intelligence – we don't yet know how it happened, but it happened. Why give this alky German minders? If the CIA had dealt with Curveball directly, they would have seen through his deceptions rather easily.

But since the information came by way of the German intelligence, the CIA tended to trust it. By the time the agency decided to take a closer look at the sourcing, war was already a done deal. Furthermore, this little scheme offered a bonus: since Tenet and McLaughlin had bought into the information from German intelligence, if it all went haywire, responsibility could be laid to rest at the feet of the CIA, not the Office of Special Plans, not the Iraqi National Congress, not German intelligence, not Mossad, not the neocon ideologues.

Once again, we see use of a bold tactic: the use of a foreign spy shop as a go-between in order to legitimise and circulate bogus (but ideologically useful) data within the US intelligence community.'

If you feed Curveball's shoddy information through German intelligence, with no CIA experts allowed to see him, and ignore the German protestations that he could not be trusted, you can have the lies fed into the American system without any caveats about reliability. The added bonus is that by using the CIA to convey the information, you can then blame the CIA when trouble erupts.

The common thread in the forged Niger documents, the use of Curveball, and the British intelligence manipulations which ended up getting David Kelly killed, is a very clever use of multiple intelligence agencies to disguise the source of a collection of rather obvious lies which were used to justify the attack on Iraq.

Whoever was behind this had to have had a long history of involvement in American government and involvement with multiple foreign intelligence agencies. There aren't that many people with that kind of experience. Who was: 1) a neocon in favour of an attack on Iraq; with 2) connections to Feith's Office of Special Plans; and with 3) ties to Chalabi and the Iraqi National Congress; and with 4) long-standing documented relationships with foreign intelligence agencies, particularly the Italians?

# Iraq and the United Nations

*Hans von Sponeck*

*Hans von Sponeck served in the United Nations for 32 years holding senior posts as UN Resident Coordinator in Botswana, Pakistan and India, Director of the UN Development Programme European Office in Geneva, and UN Humanitarian Coordinator in Iraq.*

On 2 August 1990, Iraqi troops invaded and illegally occupied Kuwait. The United Nations Security Council reacted quickly. Four days later, the most comprehensive economic and military sanctions ever pronounced against a nation were imposed on Iraq. The 1991 Gulf War forced the Iraqi Government to withdraw its troops from Kuwait. This fulfilled the conditions of resolution 661. Economic sanctions, however, were not lifted. Instead, the Security Council changed its conditions for lifting economic sanctions and decided, in April 1991, to pass resolution 687, which demanded of Iraq the disarmament of all of its weapons of mass destruction.

Throughout the years, the Security Council became increasingly disunited on the question of whether Iraq had fulfilled the disarmament requirements of resolution 687. The result was that economic sanctions remained in place until the Anglo-American invasion of Iraq, in March 2003.

Six weeks after the war, the UN Security Council formally lifted economic sanctions against Iraq, on 23 May 2003. The human conditions at that time were appalling:
i) one in five children in central and southern Iraq was chronically malnourished;
ii) mortality among children under five had plateaued after 1997 at the high level of between 100 and 120 deaths per 1000;
iii) calories per capita were at 65% of pre-sanctions levels;
iv) literacy had declined from 81% to 74%;
v) water and sanitation systems were in an extremely dilapidated state;
vi) unemployment was estimated to be between 60 and 75% of the workforce.

In 1995, the United Nations and the Government of Iraq had finally agreed on what became known as the oil-for-food programme. This followed years of confrontation over the introduction of a humanitarian exemption to protect the civilian population against the full impact of economic sanctions. It has to be asked why, despite such a humanitarian programme, socio-economic conditions were so poor in Iraq at the time sanctions were lifted, in 2003?

In 1999, the then Canadian Foreign Minister, Lloyd Axworthy, participating in an Iraq debate in the UN Security Council, made the important point that the Security Council had to act for the benefit of the international community, and not in the interest of individual member states. During the same year, the then chairman of the US Senate Foreign Relations Committee, Jesse Helms, poignantly told the UN Security Council during a visit that the United States would be ready to strengthen the United Nations 'if this was in the interest of America', and would not hesitate to do the opposite if the UN acted otherwise.

An influential group often referred to as neo-conservatives published, in 2000, a US strategy for the 21$^{st}$ century. Two years later, US President Bush formalised this position in a national security strategy document.

## The weapons of mass destruction issue took priority over humanitarian concerns

A review of the positions taken by the United States in the Security Council during the 13 years of economic sanctions and military embargo against Iraq reveal that US Government concerns rested first and foremost with Iraq's weapons of mass destruction (WMD) and US security interests, rather than with the humanitarian implications of UN Iraq policies.

US rhetoric during these years, inside and outside the UN Security Council, expressing apprehension over human conditions in Iraq cannot hide this fact. Every effort was made by Washington to prevent Iraq from re-gaining authority over its own finances, to maintain a complicated and seriously impeding UN bureaucracy for the import of supplies into Iraq under the oil-for-food programme, and to block, permanently or temporarily, goods and services from reaching the country, allegedly because of their dual-use potential.

All of this had to do with US fears that Iraq may use funds or humanitarian supplies to develop its arsenal of biological, chemical and nuclear weaponry. These fears were not unjustified given the Iraqi history of WMD production. However, had the US authorities and the UN Security Council as a whole carried out their oversight mandate more consistently and adjusted UN sanctions policies accordingly and in a timely manner, socio-economic conditions in Iraq could have developed differently and more humanely.

The UN Security Council, as an institution, left political leadership largely in the hands of its most powerful member. It also often failed to act in a timely manner, for example, in speedily raising the revenue level for the humanitarian programme in Iraq when, in 1997, the severe inadequacy of an allocation of $113 per person per year to cover all sectors of human needs (food, health, water supply and sanitation, electricity, agriculture and education) became apparent.

The Security Council recognised the ensuing damage of policies it had introduced, or individual members had unilaterally decided to follow. The

Council, however, did not have the political will or power to modify such policies. Examples include the Council's decision to deduct 30% of Iraq's oil revenue for paying compensation to foreign individuals, firms and governments that had allegedly been victimised by Iraq's invasion into Kuwait. The Security Council could easily have lowered or frozen such deductions at the time when death rates and malnutrition in Iraq were soaring.

The Council was aware that the bureaucratisation of the oil-for-food programme had introduced long delays in the arrival of humanitarian supplies. Some steps to remove such impediments were taken, but only after inordinate delays.

The Security Council was well aware that the introduction of two no-fly-zones in Iraq by the United States, United Kingdom and French governments was without international mandate and therefore illegal. Individual members of the Council intermittently raised the subject of the no-fly-zones in the Security Council. But the Council failed ever to debate these zones, even when, during 2002/03, the violations in Iraqi airspace by the United States and United Kingdom air forces had no longer even remotely to do with the protection of religious and ethnic groups such as the Shias in the south and the Kurds in the north, but instead involved deliberate destabilisation and preparation for war.

Deterioration of socio-economic conditions in Iraq certainly cannot be explained solely in terms of the negligence of the UN Security Council to carry out its oversight responsibilities, or to act in accordance with the knowledge it had of the deteriorating conditions in Iraq. The dictatorship of the Government of Saddam Hussein made its own and distinct contribution to the misery of a people.

It may be politically convenient to leave accountability for what happened in Iraq during the period up to the March 2003 war in a nebulous state of interpretation, with all the advantages this has for the stronger over the weaker party. Objective analysis, however, has to disregard a one-sided approach through which the human drama is explained by either the brutality of a regime or the failures of the international community. Much more work has to be carried out in order to fully understand the specific and separate roles the protagonists have played in bringing about the desolate conditions in Iraq.

At this stage, one can conclude that i) the economic sanctions policy has played a significant role in creating these conditions, ii) the Security Council crossed the boundary between what were unavoidable and negative side-effects of legally adopted UN sanctions and the violation of international law, including international covenants and the convention of the rights of the child, iii) the UN Security Council had more humane options but chose not to introduce these in a timely and decisive manner and thereby reduce the severity of the impact of sanctions.

## Future UN reforms – the strong must stop ignoring the weak

In the context of the re-emerging demands for the reform of the United Nations, other elements must be cited to explain Iraq sanctions policies. Among these is that the five permanent members of the Security Council had the advantage of 'permanent' association with a political issue such as sanctions against a country.

China, France, Russia, the United Kingdom and the United States were involved in the Iraq discussion from the very beginning in 1990 and throughout the years shaped Iraq policies. Process and substance of Iraq policy were in the hands of these five countries. Elected members of the Council, for example Malaysia, Bangladesh, Syria, Mexico and Canada, as involved as they were during their two-year tenure in the Council, had little chance to make a significant impact on Council policies. For many low income members it was also an issue of lacking human and financial resources that prevented a more sustained involvement. More powerful and better endowed members of the Council used this fully to their political advantage. The United Nations became like a tool box from which the powers chose what they needed at any given time, or they disregarded this box when they could not find or get the preferred implements.

The international debate leading up, in March 2003, to the invasion of Iraq can serve as a profound example of the disregard by powerful governments represented in the Security Council for positions taken by others when these questioned sanctions policies or the justification to prepare for military confrontation. The most extreme manifestation of this approach is the unilateral decision by the Governments of the United States and the United Kingdom to mount a military offensive without a UN Security Council mandate.

It has been argued before that the UN Security Council had options in the implementation of economic sanctions. The UN Security Council ultimately, however, had no options to prevent unilateral action by individual members of the Council to go to war. The two governments and their parliaments that had approved the invasion of Iraq, on the other hand, did have the options to choose what kind of a war they wanted to fight, and what kind of a peace they wanted to support afterwards. The issue that needed to be debated was not who would win this asymmetrical war. The answer was clear.

Public pronouncements showed that there was a distinct pre-occupation, as early as 2002, on the part of these two governments with the strategies and tactics of warfare, the duration and cost of the war, Iraq's military response, including the possible use of weapons of mass destruction, and the likely number of casualties within the invading armies.

Understanding Iraqi reaction to defeat, defining civilian priorities for the immediate period after the war, anticipating the response to the invasion of Shias, Sunnis and Kurds were issues either not discussed at all or considered of secondary importance. Iraqi pride in their ancient civilisation, the importance of dignity in Arab culture, local values and mores only became issues after their neglect had created an enormous backlash for the invading armies and the civil administrations that followed. At that point, the winning of the 'hearts and minds' of the Iraqis had become another battle and, as it turned out, a loosing battle.

There was a high price, first and foremost for the Iraqi people, but also for the invading armies and foreign civilian personnel, as a result of this fundamental short-sightedness. Instead of a welcome to liberators, there was armed and increasingly organised resistance to occupiers.

## Time to put pressure on the US and UK

Continental Europe, countries in the Middle East, Turkey and Russia will have to get much more and visibly involved in impressing on the governments of the United States and the United Kingdom the need to change their approach to Iraq. This should include the withdrawal of their troops. The claim that such a withdrawal would lead to civil war and the disintegration of Iraq is part of a powerful misinformation campaign. Kurds, Sunnis and Shias have co-existed for centuries. Close to a million Kurds have been living in Baghdad, making it the largest 'Kurdish' city anywhere. Shias, Sunnis, Kurds and other minorities have intermarried, lived together in mixed neighbourhoods, shared workplaces, served in the Iraqi foreign service and the military, and participated in politics. This does not mean that Iraq has been a country with total ethnic and religious harmony. There were and are ethnic and religious differences, and political confrontations have been fuelled by these differences.

The years of dictatorship witnessed the misuse of power and the victimisation of Kurdish and Shia communities. Being Kurd or Shia in itself, however, was not the cause for political persecution; opposition to Saddam Hussein and his government was. Sunnis who were working against the regime were therefore equally subjected to punishment. Occupation and external meddling harbour the distinct danger that relations between these groups will be re-defined and become more and more determined by ethnic and religious identities. *'Divide et impera'* is nothing new in political history. This lends urgency to the call for the withdrawal of foreign troops, and an end to the massive political involvement of foreign powers in Iraq's internal affairs.

To identify such demands is not difficult, to translate these into a new agenda of relationships between Iraq and the international community is. The United States and United Kingdom authorities would see this as a major political defeat, and those presently in power in Iraq as the end to their ascribed leadership. For these reasons alone there will be powerful and sustained opposition to anything that changes the present political paradigm. National and international political leaders must nevertheless have the courage and the sense of urgency to work in this direction. Otherwise, the Iraqi cataclysm will continue.

At the same time, the existing incapacity of the international machinery to handle complex issues such as the Iraq crisis must be addressed to avert a recurrence of similar crises elsewhere and to allow a comprehensive handling of terrorism. The pre-occupation with terrorists rather than with terrorism and its causes will ultimately do little to improve global security.

Large scale reforms of international structures and global application of norms relating to justice, tolerance and equal opportunity must become part of the international agenda. This points to the urgency of broad-based reforms of the United Nations. The reform debate will have to include clarification of many fundamental issues which have plagued the international community for a long time. Among them:

i) a functional division of labour between the International Court of Justice and the UN Security Council. A Security Council holding legislative, judicial and executive responsibilities, as is presently the case, produces counterproductive conflicts of interest;

ii) the enlargement of the UN Security Council.

The Commission appointed by UN Secretary General Kofi Annan has recently come up with various proposals to add permanent and non-permanent members to the existing Council of fifteen members. The proposed enlargement reminds of a refined caste-structure with various layers of permanent members, some with veto rights, others without, and non-permanent members elected to the Council for varying periods of time.

This will not be acceptable to the community of nations as it perpetuates inequality of membership. Enlargement needs to be looked at from another angle than merely more government membership. Global human security and global environment and development issues have become the top international concerns. Why could non-governmental organisations with extensive experience in these areas not become part of a reformed Security Council? The immediate and forceful rejection, especially by unilateralists, of such a proposal as utopian and therefore unworthy of consideration should not be allowed to prevent a debate.

In the context of the reform debate, the question that needs an immediate answer is: what reform steps have to be taken, by whom and when? Before this question can be answered, the international community will have to first clarify the roles international organisations such as the United Nations should be expected to play to stay relevant, what structures are needed to play these new roles, and what networks have to be created to foster peace and security.

The challenge to any reform of international structures will be the willingness of superpowers to operate within a multilateral framework and to accept international law. In the case of Iraq, it must be remembered, the United States as the dominant global power in this era decided to step outside this multilateral framework and determine its approaches on a unilateral basis. The establishment of the no-fly-zones, the December 1998 Operation Desert Fox, and the March 2003 war are straightforward examples of such unilateralism. There are less well-known examples of multilateral decision making prompted by unilateral determination. The designs of the compensation machinery to handle claims from parties victimised by Iraq's invasion into Kuwait, and the sanctions bureaucracy to manage the oil-for-food programme must be identified in this respect. Even more difficult to gauge is the unilateral forcefulness of resolution-making in the UN Security Council.

Key Iraq resolutions were seemingly 'negotiated' in the Council but, in fact, driven by individual governments, and ultimately accepted on a consensus basis by the Security Council. There have been Iraq resolutions with abstentions by permanent members, or dissenting votes by elected members, but there has not been a single resolution which was defeated by the veto of a permanent member.

This is not an example of successful diplomacy but, rather, an example of successful power politics. It furthermore demonstrates the weakness of the current multilateral machinery.

The international community has an opportunity to learn much from the case of Iraq. It can be said unequivocally that comprehensive economic sanctions are not just blunt instruments, as they have often been called. They are tools which have inflicted significant damage to innocent civilians and should not be used anymore.

Linking economic sanctions with a military embargo is holding a population responsible for the acts of their government. Such linkage, if there is genuine concern for the welfare of people who have nothing to do with a conflict, should not be introduced in the future. Instead, rigorous oversight on the part of the UN Security Council of imports into Iraq could have allowed a much more liberal inflow of goods and services needed by the population. This oversight was lacking.

The normative and structural unpreparedness of the international machinery, especially of the United Nations, to handle conflicts such as the one in Iraq, both before and after the wars of 1991 and 2003, must be fully comprehended as a first step towards remedial reforms.

Global security, a major concern for all countries, must not be seen as an issue one can handle with military might. *The priority is human not military security.* Of course, those who endanger international security, terrorists, have to be caught and brought to justice. However, in order to improve global and regional security, it is much more important to understand the causes of terrorism and act accordingly.

The agenda for reform of the international machinery for peace, conflict resolution and international development remains formidable but is achievable if all nations, including the most powerful, accept *multilateralism* as the starting point.

*References available on request.*

*With grateful acknowledgements to the Transnational Foundation for Peace and Future Research (www.transnational.org)*

© Copyright Hans von Sponeck 2005

# A Sense of Proportion

When I started to draw this picture, Homunus Corpus, the Canon of proportions, about our leader, I thought well, it's a funny thing, but he doesn't quite fit what we tend to call, in insurance lingo, the Zenith. Leonardo da Vinci wasn't sure either — a man of great perception and even greater doubt. Tony Blair, for all his faults, transformed our idea of proportion when he took over the Labour Party and added the word New. OK Well, either he is good, or, he is a complete goddamn failure. Now, I am not saying that he is, or he isn't, and sometimes I shout at him!

But, I will say that he has been a presence of some magnitude. He has made us all question just what Socialism is. Is it an Ice Cream Sundae, or is it a question forwards, backwards or sideways toward something we all thought Socialism was supposed to be, and what we all had in common? We can argue about that until the World becomes an Orange, but it is up to you. Either he is a leader — or he ain't. What I write makes no difference. What I draw may give you some idea — a sense of proportion through distortion. Ralph G the Steadman

# Countering Civil Rights

*Tony Bunyan*

*Tony Bunyan, editor of Statewatch, scrutinises the emerging counter-terrorism regime of the G8 countries and the European Union, in which 'exceptional and draconian' measures are becoming the norm. His report forms a keynote text for the 2005 Conference of the European Network for Peace and Human Rights, which meets in the European Parliament in Brussels on 20/21 October. Updates to the text will be posted on the web (www.statewatch.org).*

The United Kingdom government has replaced powers to detain suspected terrorists under the Anti-Terrorism, Crime and Security Act 2001 (ATCSA 2001) with the Prevention of Terrorism Act 2005 (PTA 2005, see Part 2).

In place of indefinite detention in Belmarsh prison, the Prevention of Terrorism Act 2005 has introduced 'control orders' which will be based on 'intelligence assessments' prepared by MI5 and authorised by the Home Secretary. 'Control orders' include 'tagging', no mobile phones or internet access, restricted movements, and indefinite 'house arrests'. Individuals will be able to appeal against the orders and conditions, but these judicial hearings will effectively take place *in camera* without the defendant or their lawyers being present.

Those who were held in Belmarsh have now all been released and put on 'control orders'. People put under 'control orders' will not be charged with a criminal offence and brought before a court and will not know the evidence against them.

The United Kingdom derogated from Article 5 of the European Convention on Human Rights – the only European Union state do so – under Part IV of the Anti-Terrorism, Crime and Security Act 2001. 'House arrests' under the new Act means it will have to derogate again. Such a derogation is only allowed where there is a 'public emergency threatening the life of the nation'. The government claims that the country is living under a permanent 'state of emergency' threatening the 'life of the nation'.

However, what is happening in the United Kingdom is indicative of other, wider developments. Behind the scenes in G8 (comprising the United States, Britain, France, Germany, Italy, Canada, Japan, Russia plus the European Union) the Council of the European Union, and the Council of Europe far-reaching changes are being planned. The first is to broaden 'terrorist offences' to cover preparatory and associated acts, even where no terrorist attack has been carried out, or even planned, and for *apologie*, condoning or sympathising with terrorism.

Second, within these broader remits, to make lawful the use of 'special investigative techniques', such as tapping, bugging, informers, bribes, undercover agents, access to all government databases (data-mining) and the sharing of this 'intelligence' with other agencies – whether inside or outside the European Union. Where 'obstacles' exist, such as requiring judicial authorisation, these should be overcome. 'Self regulation' by the agencies, with all the dangers of misuse and abuse, is to be the new norm.

Third, the intelligence gathered should be used in court while ensuring that it is 'protected'. The 'protection' of intelligence will inevitably be counter to the normal rule of law and the rights of defendants in a democracy.

The inexorable build up of 'intelligence' is fuelling these demands for new offences where people cannot now be charged and brought before the courts. The intelligence products gathered by the use of a wide range of 'special investigative techniques' will be 'protected' in court – so that the defendant will never know what the evidence is against them, where it came from, and how it was gathered.

The United States and the United Kingdom invaded Iraq together. The United States and the United Kingdom have detained people indefinitely without trial and in defiance of the rule of law. Now in a classic case of 'policy-laundering' the United States, backed by the United Kingdom, is working through the G8 group of countries to get these demands agreed in the European Union. Indeed they have offered to draw up a list of 'obstacles' to 'compliance' with them for European Union member states to overcome.

These new offences, techniques and changes in the legal process are likely to spill over into the mainstream criminal justice system and establish new norms – the discussion refers to transnational crime and crime in general. For example, nowhere is it suggested that the use of 'special investigative techniques' should be limited to tackling terrorism; 'terrorism' is simply grounds on which to legitimate their usage. What has been seen as exceptional and draconian becomes the norm.[1]

Using public and secret documents, this report looks at moves in the United Kingdom, United States, the G8, the Council of the European Union, and the Council of Europe to introduce new, preparatory offences including *apologie*, 'intelligence information' as 'evidence' in court gathered by 'special investigative techniques' including from third states, and asks can the rule of law and democratic standards survive?

## United Kingdom: From 'spin' to 'control orders'

Former Home Secretary, David Blunkett, while in India, announced proposals on 1 February 2004. He said that where 'suspected' terrorists were concerned, the government wanted to take pre-emptive action by lowering the standard of proof so that suspects could be arrested and charged before mounting an attack, and for them to be tried in secret (*in camera*) by a vetted judge. Evidence would be kept secret from the defendants so as to protect the sources of MI5, MI6 and the

Government Communications Headquarters (GCHQ), those from a third state like the United States – this would also entail 'special advocates', state-vetted defence lawyers who could be trusted not to pass on intelligence information.

As the evidence presented would come from intelligence and security sources Blunkett said that:

> 'It needs to be presented in a way that does not allow disclosure by any of the parties involved, which would destroy your security services. It is about the threshold of evidence and the nature of those involved being accredited and trusted not to reveal sources.'

The government wanted to look at the 'evidential base and the threshold of evidence'. The level of proof, Blunkett argued, could be lowered from 'beyond reasonable doubt' to the 'balance of probabilities'. He said he intended to publish his proposals in an options paper on anti-terrorist laws.

The reaction to the proposals was immediate. Baroness Helena Kennedy QC said they were 'an affront to the rule of law' and that 'he really is a shameless authoritarian'. Louise Christian, a lawyer representing a number of those held in Guantanamo Bay, said: 'I don't think he is fit to be Home Secretary'. Newspaper editorials weighed in against Blunkett's proposals; a *Guardian* editorial said that by refusing to 'seek a balance between public safety and the rule of law, he loses all sympathy'.

On 7 February 2004, six of the leading lawyers in the country, Nick Blake QC, Andrew Nicol QC, Manjit Singh QC, Ian Macdonald QC, Rick Scannell and Tom de la Mare wrote an 'open letter' condemning the proposals which:

> 'would contradict three cardinal principles of criminal justice: a public trial by an impartial judge and jury of one's peers, proof of guilt beyond reasonable doubt, and a right to know, comment on and respond to the case being made against the accused.'

David Blunkett's 'kite-flying' seemed, at the time, just that; however, it transpires that it reflected ongoing, secret discussions in the G8 (see below).

On 18 December 2003, the Privy Counsellors Review Committee published a critical report on the Anti-Terrorism, Crime and Security Act 2001 (ATCSA 2001, Part IV[2]), but the government did not respond to it.[3] The Home Secretary's proposal for pre-emptive action was not mentioned in the Home Office options paper published at the end of February 2004.[4] It did say that the internment of foreign nationals was 'essential', but that the extension of these powers to British citizens would be a big step:

> 'such draconian powers would be difficult to justify.'

The options paper did float the idea of introducing 'civil orders' against people suspected of fund-raising or propaganda work on the 'periphery' of terrorist organisations.[5]

Of direct relevance to the use of security and intelligence evidence in court – where it is provided by a third state – is a judgment given in the Court of Appeal on 11 August 2004. Considering an appeal by ten men held under the Anti-

Terrorism, Crime and Security Act 2001, the judges, by two to one, declared that the state could use evidence in court from other countries without having to investigate whether it was gathered as a result of torture or ill-treatment. The only proviso was that United Kingdom agencies should not be involved. Lord Justice Laws, one of the two in the majority, said he could not believe:

> 'he [the Home Secretary] may be presented with information of great potential importance, where there is, let us say, a suspicion as to the means by which, in another jurisdiction, it has been obtained. What is he to do?'

How could the law:

> 'sensibly impose on the Secretary of State a duty of solemn inquiry as to the interrogation methods used by agencies of other sovereign states. Apart from the practical unreality, I can find no sound juridical base for the imposition of such a requirement.'

The court of appeal had backed the government position. In the House of Lords Home Office Minister, Baroness Scotland, had told Lord Judd that:

> 'Save for evidence that is obtained from a party (usually the defendant in a criminal trial) all evidence is admissible, however unlawfully obtained.'

This view does not seem to square with the United Kingdom's ratification of the UN Convention Against Torture (Article 15) which says that:

> 'any statement which is established to have been made as a result of torture shall not be invoked as evidence in any proceedings'

Unless this judgment is overturned when it comes up on appeal in the House of Lords it will leave the door wide open to the introduction – without any questions being asked – of evidence in court gathered by torture or inhuman treatment (as long as the United Kingdom is not involved in the torture). No questions could be asked regardless of the state from which it came or the proven history of the use of such technique by the agencies of that state.

The Commissioner for Human Rights for the Council of Europe, Alvaro Gil-Robles, added his voice of opposition to internment without trial under the Anti-Terrorism, Crime and Security Act 2001 and the United Kingdom's derogation from the European Convention on Human Rights. He said he did not believe an emergency existed which could justify such powers, and that he was also concerned about police powers to detain people for up to 14 days without charge, and the disproportionate use of stop and search against Muslims. He was to issue a report on the United Kingdom in January 2005.

The judgment by the law lords (the highest court in the United Kingdom) on 16 December 2004, that detention without charge or trial is unlawful, was decided by eight to one.[6] Lord Hoffman said that what was called into question is:

> 'the very existence of an ancient liberty of which this country has until now been very proud: freedom from arbitrary arrest and detention'.

Even more damning was his conclusion that:

> 'The real threat to the life of the nation ... comes not from terrorism but from laws such as these'.

The overall view of the judges was expressed by Lady Hale who said:

> 'Executive detention is the antithesis of the right to liberty and security of the person. Yet this is what the 2001 Act allows. We have always taken it for granted that we cannot be locked up in this country without trial or explanation'.

## *'Control orders'*

On 26 January 2005, the new Home Secretary, Charles Clarke, announced in response to the law lords judgment that the government intended to replace Part 4 of the Anti-Terrorism, Crime and Security Act 2001.[7] He said that the government had considered the use of intercept material as evidence in court but some was inadmissible and some, if used, could compromise national security and its methods, damage 'relationships with foreign powers or intelligence agencies', or put 'the lives of sources at risk'.[8] He also said that the government was seeking to deport some of those held in Belmarsh prison providing 'assurances' as to their treatment could be obtained – the detained men are from Algeria, Tunisia, Egypt and Jordan[9].

Part 4 powers under the Anti-Terrorism, Crime and Security Act 2001 were replaced by the Prevention of Terrorism Act 2005 with a new system of 'control orders' covering British citizens and foreigners alike and external and internal threat of terrorism (thus covering Northern Ireland, too).[10] The Prevention of Terrorism Bill was finally passed on 11 March 2005.[11]

It took just 13 working days for parliament to pass the Act because of a government imposed timetable 'guillotine'. The final government 'compromise' is a bit complicated and is not in the Act itself. The government, in the form of the Home Secretary, said that they intended to present a new Counter-Terrorism Bill to set out 'preparatory' offences for terrorist-related activities in the autumn. It would be discussed in parliament at the same time as the first annual review of the Prevention of Terrorism Act 2005. Moreover, MPs and peers would be given parliamentary time to seek to amend the Prevention of Terrorism Act 2005. The 'compromise' is based on a 'promise'.

Article 1.3 of the Act sets out the powers 'to make control orders'. The 'Secretary of State' (ie: the Home Secretary) is empowered to make an order against an individual and set out the conditions (eg: tagging) for suspected 'terrorist related activity'. The range of 'control orders' is set out in Clause 1.4 and includes:
– prohibition of having 'specified articles' in their possession (eg: a mobile phone)
– prohibition of having access to 'specified services' (eg: the internet)
– restriction on work or occupation
– restriction of 'association' with 'specified persons' or 'other persons generally'
– restriction on place of residence and who can visit
– restriction on movement to an area or region
– restriction on movement *'to, from or within the United Kingdom'* (including

surrendering passport)
- to give access at all times of 'specified persons' (police and Special Branch) to residence
- to allow searches at any times of the residence[12] plus being required to wear a 'tag' and – 'house arrest' (Clause 1.5)

Charles Clarke, the Home Secretary, has admitted that control orders could result in a similar scenario with the family and friends of the individual being subject to the same constraints.[13]

Control orders (of both kinds) can be imposed for 12 months and can be renewed on 'one or more occasions'. There is nothing to stop control orders from becoming virtually permanent. If a person breaks the conditions of an order they can be sent to prison for up to five years without there being any further judicial examination of the case against them – they can be sent to prison without a trial taking place.

These sixteen conditions are termed 'non-derogating', though Ben Emmerson QC argues that a combination of control orders would constitute a breach of the Convention.[14] A 'derogating control order' (from the European Convention on Human Rights) is where a person is placed under 'house arrest' (1.5). The issuing of 'non-derogating' control orders is simply based on 'reasonable grounds for suspecting' a person is involved in terrorist-related activities. The judiciary then has to confirm the order, but within very restricted conditions which are a far cry from a judge-made decision. The government is only obliged to show the judge sufficient 'intelligence' to convince them of the need for a control order (not the whole intelligence dossier). The role of the judges is defined as being governed by the rules of a 'judicial review', which is not at all the same as a full hearing of all the evidence and then the judge making the decision.

In effect the judiciary will be asked to confirm the decision of the minister and can only overturn both the decision and the conditions imposed if they are: 'obviously flawed'. In other words, the judiciary can only reject the minister's decision if there is absolute evidence that it is wrong. It is no wonder that the judiciary are concerned that they will be caught up in a process for which they will take part of the blame.

At the initial hearing – when a non-derogating or derogating order has been issued by the minister – the court can hear the application without the suspect being present (3.5.a), without the suspect even having been notified (3.5.b), and without the accused being given the opportunity of making any representation to the court (3.5.c).

For derogating control orders the initial hearing – on a application by the minister – only has to agree that there are 'reasonable grounds for believing' it is necessary. Also at this initial hearing the hands of the judges are also tied because a control order can be issued where:

> 'there is material which (if not disproved) is capable of being relied on by the court as establishing that the individual is or has been involved in terrorism-related activity (4.3.a).'

It is very hard to see how the 'material' could be 'disproved' as the person will not be present, will not know the evidence against them, and will not be represented. It is only at the first full hearing that the judgment will be based on the 'balance of probabilities'.

The Schedule to the Act sets out the details of the court proceedings. A judge must ensure that:

> 'disclosures of information are not made where they would be contrary to the national interest' (Section 11.2).

The 'rules of court' will be drawn up by the Lord Chancellor (Section 11.3). These 'rules of court' include 'the mode of proof', enabling or requiring proceedings to be determined without a hearing (Section 11.4.1).

Most crucially the 'rules of court' can makes provisions for control order proceedings or appeals:

> 'to take place without the full particulars of the reasons for the decisions to which the proceedings relate being given to a relevant party to the proceedings or his legal representative' (Section 11.4.2a).

The proceedings can also take place in 'the absence' of the person concerned and their lawyer (Section 11.4.2b). The person will only receive a 'summary of evidence taken in his absence' (Section 11.4.2.d). This 'summary' is to be prepared by the Home Secretary. The Home Secretary is to give the hearings all 'relevant material' – which, of course, may only be that necessary to convince rather than the full 'intelligence assessment' provided by MI5, on which the initial decision was taken.

The 'interests' of the 'suspect' are to be 'represented' by special advocates, appointed by the Attorney-General, who will not be allowed to communicate with the 'suspect' or their lawyers (Section 11.7).

'Terrorist-related' activity is defined in Article 1.9 as the 'commission, preparation or instigation of acts of terrorism' (which it might be thought would already be criminal offences) or 'conduct which gives support or assistance to individuals who are known or believed to be involved in terrorist-related activity' or:

> 'conduct which gives **encouragement** to the commission, preparation or instigation of such acts, or which is intended to do so' (emphasis added).

The term 'encouragement' is not defined. The scope of the term 'encouragement' is compounded by the overall provision for Clause 1.9 which says it is:

> 'immaterial whether the acts of terrorism in question are specific acts of terrorism of acts of terrorism in general.'

The proposed offence of 'encouragement' for 'acts of terrorism generally' is suspiciously close to the highly contentious concept of '*apologie*' being proposed in the Council of Europe draft Convention on Terrorism which could endanger free speech and freedom of the press (see below).

Under the Prevention of Terrorism Act 2005, all meaningful proceedings will take place *in camera* (press and public excluded), without the defendant present – who will thus not know the evidence against him, nor will his lawyer.

The differences between judicial scrutiny and normal criminal procedure are important. If an individual is formally charged with terrorist offences the trial would be before a judge and jury and the defendant would know the evidence against him. Some evidence may be presented in camera with the public excluded and witnesses may appear by video link or give evidence from behind a screen to protect their identity. On the other hand, 'independent judicial scrutiny' means a hearing before a judge(s) but no jury. The defendant and his lawyers will not hear or see the evidence. The only people to hear the evidence will be the judge and the 'special advocates' appointed by the Attorney-General to try and put forward the views of the defendant, and they are not allowed to tell the defendant what the evidence is against him or ask him for his views to contradict the 'evidence'.

One of the arguments advanced by Charles Clarke, the Home Secretary, and by John Denham, ex-Home Minister and chair of the Home Affairs Select Committee, is that other countries in the European Union can hold people suspected of terrorist activities for up to four years. This is a disingenuous argument. It is true that countries such as Spain and Germany, for example, can hold people in 'preventive detention', usually for up to two years in Germany and three years in Spain. In Spain people may be held where: 1) there is a danger that the person may flee, 2) or that they may destroy evidence, or 3) that they may repeat the alleged offence. The same goes for Germany where people can also be held for suspected participation in a terrorist organisation. But, and this is the crucial difference, in both countries:

a) 'preventive detention' can only be ordered by a judge
b) the defendant can appoint a lawyer of their choice
c) the state has to present sufficient evidence in court to justify detention – the defendant knows the evidence against them
d) the defence can question the evidence and the grounds for detention (eg: fleeing).

This is a judicial process, in a court with evidence presented to the defendant which can be questioned, and the defendant has full rights – not a decision by a government minister.

As the first control orders were issued it emerged that private security firms were to be responsible for carrying out some of the surveillance of the individuals. The Home Office's 'Regulatory Assessment' of the costs of the Act says:

> 'There will be costs to the police/Home Office in terms of monitoring the Orders but where possible these will be contracted out to private companies as per existing arrangements. Systems are already in place for monitoring criminals released on licence and other offenders'[15]

And the experience of those placed under control orders imposes an almost life on them and their families.[16]

## *The use of 'intelligence information'*
'Control orders' are to be based, Charles Clarke told parliament:

> 'on the basis of an intelligence assessment provided by the Security Service [where] there are reasonable grounds for suspecting that an individual is, or has been, concerned with terrorism'

which means that *all sources of intelligence* can be included – whether from the United Kingdom or external sources (such as the United States).

When the Home Secretary made a statement on 26 January 2005, a number of MPs asked why intercept evidence (that is, from telephone-tapping) could not be used in court? This could ensure that a person could be formally charged and brought before a criminal court. A number of newspaper editorials and individuals pursued the same line of argument. It is also being 'pedalled' in the media that 'intercept evidence' is allowed in other European countries so why not here, too? Javier Solana, the High Representative of the Council of the European Union, said the same during an ITV television interview by Jonathan Dimbleby, and said that not to use intercept material was 'naive' (6.2.05).[17]

However, when the United Kingdom Home Secretary talks about getting an 'intelligence assessment' from MI5 (Security Service), he is *not* talking just about phone 'intercept' evidence.[18] The Home Secretary is talking about a range of 'intelligence evidence' on which he would base a decision to issue a control order from a variety of sources including:
– telephone conversations from fixed phones and mobile phones (including the locations of both parties), plus text messages
– faxes
– e-mails (including the location of both parties) with both traffic data and full contents of the communications
– 'bugging' (covert listening device) and video evidence
– internet usage (web sites visited and pages/files downloaded)
– from tracking devices on vehicles and/or people and/or an object containing a tracking device
– surveillance photos and video
– reports and statements from covert sources (informers or undercover agents) of varying degrees of reliability and accuracy (judged on a scale of 1-5).
– open source material (such as press cuttings)
– employment, bank, credit card, health records, vehicle and insurance details
– travel details, especially to and from 'dubious' states and/or regarding suspect individuals/groups
– membership or association with 'suspect' organisations
– in addition all of the above from a European Union agency (eg: Europol and/or SitCen) or member state agencies
– in addition all of the above from non-European Union state agencies (eg: the United States), which may include statements gathered through the use of torture and ill-treatment, and sources/witnesses would not be available for cross-

examination.

It is for this reason that the government wants to retain the power to issue an executive order (control order) rather than cede this initial decision to a court. Equally they are assuming that in the closed hearings of a judicial review only a fraction of the underlying intelligence would have to be revealed – just sufficient 'evidence' to convince. This view is confirmed in the Bill (Schedule 4.3.c) which states that the Secretary of State does not have to disclose 'anything' which will not be relied on in court.

The introduction of intelligence as 'evidence' presents major problems and consequences. Would, for example, evidence of an intercepted phone conversation include all the conversations or just the one singled out by the security agencies? Would the full text of the intercept be available to the court and the defence or just selections from it? Would a statement from an unnamed source, probably called person 'A', (ie: an informer or infiltrated agent or a person being held in custody) be acceptable? Would the defence be allowed to question the source? How could the defence question a statement if the origin was from outside the United Kingdom, for example, from the United States, Saudi Arabian or Egyptian agencies? The question of evidence gathered through the use of torture has yet to be considered by the law lords.[19]

Four British men held in Gauntanamo Bay for over three years were released in January 2005. On their return to the UK they were questioned by anti-terrorist police, then released without charge a day later. However, the men have now been told by the Home Secretary that they pose a terrorist threat to the United Kingdom, and that they are banned from travelling abroad, and are to be denied passports.[20] In a letter to them the Home Secretary states:

> 'On the basis of the information which has come to light during your detention by the United States, the Home Secretary considered that there are strong grounds for believing that, on leaving the United Kingdom, you would take part in activities against the United Kingdom or allied targets.'

The men and their lawyers say that any admissions made while being held in Guantanamo Bay are false and were made under duress (ranging from torture to ill-treatment). On the basis of 'intelligence' supplied by the United States the men have been denied the freedom of movement.

'Control orders' could be used by the security agencies (MI5 and the Special Branch) to target 'activist' or suspected 'ringleaders' and result in dozens of Muslims being criminalised. Already the agencies use the Terrorism Act 2000, the Anti-Terrorism, Crime and Security Act 2001, and stop and search powers to 'disrupt' suspected groups against whom they have no evidence of a terrorist offence.[21]

At present the United Kingdom is the only country in the European Union which has chosen to take exceptional measures. But behind the scenes a new agenda is being set by the G8 which will affect the whole of the European Union.

## How the G8 is setting the agenda

The United Kingdom Home Secretary's proposals, back in February 2004, did not happen simply by chance. The origin of these proposals came from a much higher source – the G8, where Home Office, MI5 and MI6 officials are key players (alongside the United States).[22]

The role of the G8 took on a new dimension after 11 September 2001. It is a 'global' grouping which can set global standards. Two of its first demands were for international standards for biometrics on passports, and the retention of telecommunications traffic data – the first of which has been agreed by the European Union and the second is now going through its legislative process – neither, as yet, has even been proposed in the United States. Another was for checking and surveillance of all visitors entering a country – the United States has introduced this, and the European Union is about to (commonly known as checking 'PNR', Passenger Name Records, against 'watch-lists').[23] It is also of relevance to note four G8 members already intern/detain people without charge and trial – the United States, United Kingdom, Russia and Canada.[24]

As the ideology of the 'war on terrorism' deepened and became permanent, other standards were set out by the G8. Notable in this context are the G8 recommendations on transnational crime which were 'endorsed' by the G8 Ministers of Justice and Interior Ministers at Mont-Tremblant in Canada on 13-14 May 2002.[25] Although referring to 'transnational crime', the recommendations were directed at 'transnational crime and terrorism'.[26]

Among the key recommendations is a section on 'strengthening investigative capabilities', including 'Investigative techniques'. Even among the G8 countries, let alone the European Union and the rest of the world, the use of telephone-tapping, bugging and video surveillance, informers, *agent-provocateurs,* and undercover agents is stringently circumscribed in law – in many European Union countries judicial authorisation is required to carry out covert surveillance.[27]

For example, in seven European Union states the police require judicial authorisation to access 'documentation of telephone tapping' and in a further nine states they cannot obtain this information without judicial authorisation. For 'documentation of room bugging' eight states require judicial authorisation to access it and in a further nine states they cannot obtain this information without judicial authorisation. In nine states 'real-time' telecom monitoring requires judicial authorisation to access and in fourteen states they do this without judicial authorisation. As to access to traffic data held by service providers, in nine states the police require judicial authorisation, and thirteen states cannot obtain this information without judicial authorisation. 'Judicial authorisation' is seen within the G8 plans as an 'obstacle' to efficient cooperation between agencies – both internally and externally.

The use of such investigative techniques is perceived as being exceptional and their everyday use associated with authoritarian states. In May 2002 this G8 meeting agreed on:

'the relevance and effectiveness of special investigative techniques such as electronic or other forms of surveillance technology, undercover operations and controlled deliveries.'[28]

G8 states were called on to review their:

'domestic arrangements for those techniques, also ensuring any necessary anonymity of undercover agents and to conclude, where necessary, appropriate bilateral and multilateral agreements and arrangements for using the special investigative techniques in the context of cooperation at international level...'

This commitment is immediately followed by the following recommendation:

'We emphasise the importance of giving the fullest possible protection to sensitive information received from other states. The competent authorities of different states should advise each other as to the requirements regarding the disclosure of information in the course of judicial and administrative proceedings, and discuss in advance potential difficulties arising from those requirements.'

From this point on there is an ongoing link between 'special investigative techniques' and how to allow the product of surveillance to be used – whether by other 'friendly' agencies or in 'judicial proceedings'.[29]

The meeting of G8 Ministers of Justice and Home Affairs in Paris on 5 May 2003 (prior to the Evian G8 Summit) reiterated the need to 'promote special investigative techniques' and called on their 'experts' to 'identify the obstacles' to international judicial cooperation in this area.

## United States takes over the Presidency of G8

The United States took over the Presidency of G8 on 1 January 2004 and sent out a questionnaire to its member states drawn up by the 'Roma Group'.

On 23 February 2004, there was a European Union-United States high-level officials meeting on justice and home affairs under the 'New Transatlantic Agenda', held in Dublin. The Irish Presidency Chair of the European Union's Article 36 Committee, assisted by officials, met with their US counterparts. The meeting was an: 'EU-US Troika JHA Informal/SCIFA Informal Troika' (Troika refers to past, present and next EU presidency).[30] The report on the meeting is peppered with references to on-going work in G8 (of which neither Ireland nor the next EU Presidency, Netherlands, are members).[31]

At the meeting, the United States took the lead on the topic of 'Terrorism prevention measures' and 'expressed three concerns regarding [EU Member] States abilities to fight terrorism':

'The first concern was that states' legal systems should allow their law enforcement authorities to take action against preparatory acts for terrorism at a stage where no terrorist acts had been committed.'

The second US concern was the ability of European Union states to:

'afford mutual legal assistance and extradite persons for preparatory acts.'

While the third:

> 'probably most difficult issue which was raised by the US was how to share intelligence information related to terrorism for use in a criminal proceeding in another country, while ensuring that the intelligence would be protected.
>
> This question is two-pronged: (1) have states the legal ability to protect intelligence information, and (2) how can the (prosecutorial) authorities of a state be informed of the fact that another state holds intelligence information which is relevant to the terrorist case that is being prosecuted. The US clearly signalled that it was seeking to cooperate with the EU and its Member States on this issue. As a first step it suggested drawing up a document that would collate information from the US and the Member States, which would lay out to what extent and how states can protect intelligence information received from another country.
>
> The G8 had already started work on this by way of a questionnaire that had been sent out to and replied by all G8 members. The US suggested that the EU might consider following up on this questionnaire in relation to use of intelligence information.'

In summation the United States said that:
1. law enforcement agencies should be 'allowed' to take action against preparatory acts for terrorism where no such act has been committed.
2. extradition should be allowed for 'preparatory acts'.
3. intelligence 'information' should be used in court while ensuring it is 'protected'.

Even as the United States was canvassing the European Union to support these ideas, it was preparing to put a series of issues openly and explicitly on the table at the G8 meeting of Justice and Home Affairs Ministers in Washington on 11 May 2004 – it should be remembered that of the now 25 European Union member states only the United Kingdom, France, Italy and Germany have a say (the European Commission is also in attendance).

The press release from the Washington meeting again linked the use of 'advanced investigative techniques' with the 'sharing' of intelligence to:

> 'better prevent and disrupt terrorist activities and to prosecute terrorists.'

There were three detailed recommendations on:
– 'special investigative techniques'[32];
– 'enhancing the legal framework to prevent terrorist attacks'[33];
– protecting intelligence in prosecutions.[34]

The Lyon and Roma groups, under the French and United States G8 Presidencies, had conducted a survey of 'special investigative techniques' which led to the recommendation that 'legal systems' should 'allow' the use of techniques such as:

> 'use of undercover agents, use of covert filing and listening devices, and covert interception of all forms of electronic communications.'

Seven recommendations follow including:

a. the use of 'special investigative techniques to support *criminal proceedings* at national and international levels' (emphasis added)
b. the creation of a 'legal framework' which allows the use of '*special investigative techniques*'
c. 'access to a broad array of special investigative techniques for the purpose of international investigation'
d. here the recommendation (no 6) makes a direct link between the use of the 'techniques' and the use of their product in court:

> 'Requested States should work with requesting States to maximise the likelihood of admissibility in the requesting State of evidence provided through special investigative techniques.

The mere fact that a special investigative technique, carried out by the requested State in accordance with its law, would not be available to the requesting State in similar circumstances, *should not per se bar the use of evidence so acquired in the requesting State's courts*' (emphasis added).

This could mean, for example, that the United States could request a European Union state to conduct blanket electronic surveillance of a particular group based in the European Union and this 'intelligence' could be used in the United States where this power may not exist (or, at least, not the power to produce such intelligence 'intercepts' by US agencies in its courts). Similarly, it covers tapes or statements from people held in states where the use of torture or inhuman treatment in suspected terrorist cases is the norm.

The second recommendation covers creating a 'legal framework to prevent terrorist attacks'. The emphasis here is on people and groups suspected of preparatory acts requiring action in:

> 'situations in which the terrorist objective is not yet well defined and an attack may not happen for some time... prevention, investigation and prosecution are complimentary in nature...'

The objective is to take action against people and groups 'prior to terrorist attacks being carried out'. What this means is not spelt out. Does this refer to people who are buying, gathering and collecting materials which could be used in an attack? If so, this would be understandable. Does it mean people with 'radical' views, who may have visited Pakistan or Afghanistan in the past and who consort with others, some of whom have done the same? If so, this would be unacceptable.

The recommendation calls for criminal offences covering 'recruiting persons to commit terrorist acts' (which is clear) and providing 'directly or indirectly' financial or other 'material support' and:

> 'a person who engages in such conduct should be criminally liable not only where he or she knows or intends that the conduct will facilitate the commission of a specific attack, but also where he or she knows or intends that the conduct will facilitate the commission of future unspecified attacks.'

The latter category is not clear. Does the giving of a mobile phone to someone constitute such conduct? The person may have 'radical views' but in giving the phone how is intention to be judged? Does the giving of a pair of boots, which end up in Chechnya in the hands of a suspected Al Qaeda group, constitute giving 'material support'?[35]

Another recommendation specifically refers to social, religious and charitable groups who should also be subject to 'special investigative techniques':

> 'while duly respecting established legal privileges recognised under domestic law, such as attorney-client or clergyman-penitent confidentiality and respect for diplomatic status, the fact of involvement of entities whether social, religious or charitable in nature, or of their leaders should not per se bar use of investigative techniques.'

This set of recommendations calls for i) the use of bribes ('incentives') to gather intelligence; ii) those defined above as 'directly or indirectly' suspected of giving material support to be extraditable for 'anticipatory or preparatory' offences; iii) states should 'assist another country' by conducting 'a broad array of special investigative techniques' against targets at their request.

The third set of recommendations covers the use of 'intelligence' gathered through 'special investigative techniques' in the 'prosecution of terrorists and their associates' while giving:

> 'appropriate protection to national security intelligence information in criminal prosecutions.'

The recommendations call on states to:

1. 'adopt legislation' and 'procedural safeguards' to 'prevent, disrupt and pre-empt' terrorist activities by permitting:

> 'information sharing among and between their intelligence community, their law enforcement community and their prosecutors, to the fullest possible degree.'

2. 'adopt legislation' to establish 'procedural safeguards' which will:

> 'permit national security intelligence information to be used in the prosecution of terrorists and those who commit associated offences, while protecting such information, including sources and methods by which such information has been acquired; *to the extent possible* consistent with a fair trial, such mechanisms, for example, include the use of summaries, substitutions or stipulations' (emphasis added).

What is meant by 'summaries'? It implies that the agencies will be able to present an edited version of an intercept or statement from an informer? Does 'substitution' mean getting rid of juries and introducing judge-only 'Diplock' courts? And does 'stipulations' mean that defence lawyers will have to be vetted and defendants not allowed to see the 'evidence' against them?

3. 'adopt legislation' allowing: 'national security intelligence information' from a third state to be 'used in a criminal proceeding' subject to:

'the conditions, if any, agreed upon between the competent authorities in the originating State and those in the receiving State'

If 'legislation' to this effect were adopted the 'conditions' agreed between intelligence agencies would override the power of the courts to decide otherwise.

4. in 'adopting' this 'legislation' states should:

'give due regard to civil liberties and fundamental principles of law.'

Well, enough said.

Taken together these recommendations would totally undermine any concept of a fair trial and the presumption of innocence. They would 'legalise' the pre-emptive detention of those held in Belmarsh who are being held on unseen 'evidence' provided by United Kingdom intelligence and security agencies.[36]

The G8 Sea Island Summit in the United States on 8-10 June 2004 simply noted the recommendations from the Justice and Home Affairs Ministers in Washington on 11 May 2004.

The United States handed over Presidency of the G8 to the United Kingdom on 1 January 2005.

## The European Union-United States Summit at Dromoland Castle, Ireland on 26 June 2004

It might be thought that the 25 member states in the European Union could act independently of its four G8 members – the United Kingdom, Germany, France and Italy. After all, only the United Kingdom had attempted to 'pre-empt' alleged terrorist activity by imprisoning seventeen men under its Anti-Terrorism, Crime and Security Act 2001 without trial – and is the only European Union member state to derogate from Article 5 of the European Convention on Human Rights.

However, at the European Union-United States Summit in Ireland on 26 June 2004 the 'European Union-United States Declaration on combating terrorism' agreed to 'take forward... objectives, through dialogue and action at all levels' including twelve 'objectives' to 'detect, investigate and prosecute terrorists and prevent terrorist attacks'.[37] The wording in the Declaration will seem familiar by now and includes:

'3.3 We will work together to enhance, in accordance with national legislation, our abilities to share information among intelligence and law enforcement agencies to prevent and disrupt terrorist activities, and to better use sensitive information as allowed by national legislation in aid of prosecutions of terrorists in a manner which protects the information, while ensuring a fair trial' [European Union doc no: 10809/04]

There should be:
– 'appropriate legislation in place to investigate and prosecute *offences linked to terrorist activities*' (3.4)

– A new criminal offence of 'knowingly supplying or attempting to supply material or logistic support' should be created (3.5).
– The use of 'investigative techniques' should be promoted (3.6)
– and 'proposals directed at improving the exchange of personal information for the purposes of combating terrorism' will be regularly reviewed (3.7).
– Cooperation between 'US prosecutors and Eurojust' should be strengthened (3.9)
– the European Union-United States agreements on extradition and mutual legal assistance should be 'rapidly' completed so that joint investigation teams and 'enhanced cooperation' (eg: including requests for surveillance and intercepts from the USA) can be effected (3.10).

And, finally, there should be improved:

> 'co-operation on the sharing of law enforcement and other sensitive information between government agencies consistent with national legislation, and the need to protect sources and fair procedures' (3.12).

The swift endorsement by the European Union of the central demands of the G8 and the United States comes as no surprise to observers who have watched the extensive build-up of European Union-United States cooperation and high-level meetings on justice and home affairs since the beginning of 2002 – evidence of the emerging United States-European Union 'axis' on the 'war on terrorism' (as distinct from their differences on the war against the 'axis of evil').

The Dromoland Declaration was followed up at the 'European Union-United States Justice and Home Affairs Informal High Level' meeting at Wassenaar, Netherlands on 7 July 2004. The United States side 'emphasised that not every item in the Declaration could be finalised' quickly and that 'it was advisable to prioritise' – there were 42 points in the Declaration. The third 'priority' point was 'Preparatory (anticipatory crime)':

> 'The US raised the issue of joint EU-US forces aiming at a systematic approach to prevent terrorist acts. The US was interested in adopting and implementing a prevention strategy, defining minimum level provisions on crimes in preparation, legal competence on mutual legal assistance and extradition and a more difficult issue, the sharing of information subject to data protection.'

The minutes of the meeting state: 'The questionnaire on the use of intelligence in criminal court cases was discussed' and 'The [Netherlands] Presidency concluded that the European Union and the United States would cooperate as agreed in the EU-US Declaration.'

## The European Union initiative is launched

Just three weeks after the High Level European Union-United States meeting in Wassenaar, on 28 July 2004, the Netherlands Presidency of the Council sent a questionnaire to the Working Party on Substantive Criminal Law for member states to respond to by 1 September 2004.[38]

The reason for the circulation of the 'Questionnaire on prevention of terrorism' was because:

> 'the US authorities have conveyed several concerns regarding States' abilities to fight terrorism.
> 
> A first concern relates to the ability of law enforcement authorities to take action against preparatory acts for terrorism at a stage where no terrorist acts had been committed. A second concern related to the ability of states to afford mutual legal assistance and extradite persons for preparatory acts. The third issue which has been raised by the US is how to share intelligence information related to terrorism for use in criminal proceedings in another country, while ensuring that the intelligence is protected.'

It should come as no surprise that the questionnaire sent out to the 25 European Union member states was the same questionnaire already answered by all G8 members. The questionnaire is primarily directed at the first and third of the United States' 'concerns' – the introduction of a preparatory criminal offence and the protection of intelligence information in court proceedings. It opens by asking if it is a crime in their countries to 'incite or recruit' for terrorist acts (A.1) and to provide 'directly or indirectly' material support (A.2).

The next question (A.3) makes explicit the distinction between current criminal offences directed at acts committed or knowingly of the planned commission of a terrorist act and the new concept of 'preparatory' or 'associated' offences. The questionnaire asks:

> 'Can liability also arise where there is a more general mental state, such as where the recruiter/inciter/supporter intends to, or knows that his or her conduct will aid future unspecified terrorist acts?'

It is also asked whether there are legal limits on action against religious leaders or charitable institutions (A.4) and whether financial inducements before an attack or after are lawful?

The second series of questions opens with the use of 'special investigative techniques' (B.1), including:

> 'can the government overtly or covertly observe conduct taking place in a house of worship or property otherwise belonging to a religious or charitable entity? Can electronic surveillance be conducted in such a location? Are there limitations to executing searches and seizures in such a location?'

It goes on to ask whether a 'religious figure' can be lawfully questioned or information gathered about them, and do any 'legal privileges' bar gathering such information of evidence? (B.2) And are there any legal limits on detaining or arresting religious figures? (B.3)

The question on the use of 'intelligence' in court (B.4) follows:

> 'To what extent do you have procedures under your law that permit the use in judicial proceedings of national security intelligence information in a manner that protects its source while adequately protecting rights of the defence?'

The final question asks whether a European Union state can assist a non-European Union state (for example, the United States) in:

> 'gathering information and evidence by other countries for use in their criminal investigations or prosecutions?'

It then explicitly uses as an example the surveillance and bugging of a place of worship.

The term 'mutual legal assistance' is a euphemism for acts such as this. For example, can the United States request that a European Union member state either place a targeted person(s) under surveillance and give the intelligence 'product' to them or, as the above phraseology suggests, allowing (and aiding) US agencies to carry out the surveillance of the 'target(s)?'[39]

## – *The response to the European Union questionnaire*

As far as can be ascertained only 11 out of 25 European Union member states have responded to the questionnaire. Some member states responded by setting out the current legal situation in their countries with little further comment (for example, Germany and Portugal).[40] A number of member states said that the Framework Decision on combating terrorism (13.6.02) already covered terrorist acts including preparatory and accessory acts.

Slovakia said:

> 'Its practical use would be improved if the American party could be confronted with the same questions too.'

The Czech Republic said the same.

Belgium, Ireland and Austria thought it would be 'very useful' if the European Union G8 members were to inform the rest of the European Union of their responses. It also proposed that any questionnaire should be drafted by all the parties so that each could make amendments and that information should be shared between all the partners – including the United States.

Greece was not convinced that these 'American style' measures were needed and wanted to know how intelligence information could be protected. It was concerned, too, over lack of mention of the European Convention on Human Rights, reciprocity, the death penalty, and data protection.

Austria expressed strong concerns about a 'shift' in what is perceived as criminal which could put the rights of suspects at risk and infringe freedom of religious expression. For example, the line between the procurement of intelligence information and its use in prosecutions not revealing sources.

Germany was the only European Union member of the G8 to supply the same answers to the questionnaire as it gave to the G8 – a basic statement of the current legal position in Germany.

The United Kingdom's response – which did not include its response to the G8 questionnaire – is very revealing. The United Kingdom's view is that the questions are 'pertinent to the concerns of the United States' and that:

> 'the burden of completing such questionnaires can be considerable, and we wonder whether this is the most cost-effective means of addressing this issue.

It might be preferable for the G8 to put forward a set of preliminary proposals and invite European Union Member States to comment on them, including the extent to which they are already compliant and any legal or other impediments they foresee to their becoming compliant.'

In other words, the United Kingdom's view is that the G8 should be in charge of initiating these proposals and that European Union member states should set out any problems with becoming *'compliant'* to its demands. There could not be a clearer expression of how the United Kingdom views the European Union and how the 'Atlantic Alliance' of the United Kingdom and the United States reflects their dominant role within G8.

The Council's Working Party on Substantive Criminal Law discussed the issue at its meeting on 8-9 September 2004 and a 'number of delegations' asked for clarification as to the aim of the questionnaire. 'Certain delegations' also asked for the distribution of the responses of European Union members of the G8 to its questionnaire. The matter was referred upwards to the Article 36 Committee.

The high-level Article 36 Committee discussed the issue at its meeting on 7-8 October 2004 and concluded that the Presidency should contact the United States to see how it 'would like to proceed' and ask for a copy of the US reply to the G8 questionnaire (European Union states in G8 should also make their responses available). This response might seem to indicate a luke-warm response to the United States (and United Kingdom) demand. However, the influence of top Justice and Home Affairs officials in the Council (and Commission) who meet and discuss with their United States counterparts regularly, and who take part in G8 working groups, should not be under-estimated.

## Council of the European Union takes up the initiative

The proposal for using intelligence information as evidence in court was raised within the closed circles of the Council of the European Union in an unreleased review of its work to combat terrorism early in 2004. This report from the Council's General Secretariat to COREPER (the committee of permanent representatives of the member states based in Brussels) said:

'One of the main problems to be addressed is the use of intelligence as evidence in courts in full respect of the right of defence.'

In an 'evaluation report' by Mr Vries, the European Union Counter-Terrorism Coordinator (based in the Council), produced at the end of May 2004, asks:

'How can intelligence be exploited so that it can be used, if necessary, by courts in legal proceedings?' [EU doc no: 9876/04] [41]

A 'more integrated approach' is 'desirable' to the sharing of information between different state databases (for example, police and customs) and it should be considered whether:

'security services could also have a permanent access to law enforcement databases and to other relevant administrative databases, such as border management ones.'

The report also noted that some internal security services had legal powers for the 'interception of communications or eavesdropping' while:

> 'In some Member States, there is no specific legal framework relating to special investigative techniques.'

The updated 'EU Plan of Action on Combating Terrorism' agreed at the European Union Summit (meeting of prime ministers) in December 2004 reflected developments on some of the issues raised in this analysis (doc no: 16090/04). Two of the seven overall 'Objectives' are pertinent.

Objective 3 is 'to maximise capacity within European Union bodies and Member States to detect, investigate and prosecute terrorists and prevent attacks'. These measures include three measures already in the pipeline: i) a draft Council Decision on the exchange of information and cooperation concerning terrorist offences (Council doc no: 15871/04); ii) a draft Decision on the exchange of information extracted from the criminal record (Council doc no: 15281/04); iii) a draft Framework Decision on simplifying the exchange of information and intelligence between the law enforcement authorities of Member States particularly in respect of serious crimes including terrorist acts (original proposal from Sweden, doc on:10215/04) – this is referred to as introducing the 'principle of availability' as endorsed by the 'Hague Programme' (4.11.04). This 'Objective' contains no reference to the introduction of intelligence evidence in court proceedings nor of 'special investigative techniques'.[42]

Objective 6 'to address factors which contribute to support for, and recruitment into, terrorism' was added in the June 2004 version of the Action Plan (doc no: 10010/3/04, after 11 March bombings). The June and December Action Plans (2004) contain under this Objective:

> 'conduct more detailed studies, including academic studies, of recruitment to terrorism in specific contexts such as prisons, in schools, in universities or in mosques; studies into the role of the media, including the internet, in radicalisation or in promoting support or sympathy for terrorists...' (6.1.3)

Another point concerns investigating 'links between extreme religious or political beliefs ... and support for terrorism'. The December 2004 Action Plan now assigns this task to SitCen (the European Union's Situation Centre) to include relevant material in its 'assessments'.[43]

The concept of 'radicalisation and recruitment' is now widely used in European Union justice and home affairs documents.[44] The Action Plan notes that: 'countering radicalisation and recruitment needs a joint strategy of police and security services'. The first ever meeting of the Council's Counter Terrorism Group (CTG) and the Police Chiefs Task Force (PCTF) led to a report making recommendations 'to better structure the process of intelligence-gathering'.

A report on 'recruitment to terrorism' has been completed – though this is not public (6.1.1). However the *European Voice* newspaper reports (9.12.04) that a report drawn up after the discussions between the (CTG) and PCTF identifies mosques, the internet and prisons as 'hot spots' for the recruitment to 'extremists' by terrorist groups. It recommends that national security services should increase their intelligence-gathering at such locations and that Europol should undertake more 'profiling' of 'Islamic extremists'.

## The role of the European Union's Counter-Terrorism Coordinator

Mr Gijs de Vries was appointed by the Council as the 'Counter-Terrorism Coordinator' after the bombings in Madrid on 11 March 2004. One of de Vries' jobs has been to conduct evaluation of 'national anti-terrorism arrangements' and to make 'recommendations' which 'may presuppose amendments or adjustments of existing legal or structural arrangements'.[45] The 'interim report' of the Coordinator (23 November 2004) makes a series of 'recommendations' and then 'additional suggestions' based on the evaluation reports. His second recommendation concerns the security services and 'information sharing':

> 'In order to detect, identify and facilitate profiling at a very early stage terrorists, terrorist networks and individuals supporting them as well as their plans and activities [there should be] access to law enforcement and other relevant administrative or government agencies databases (eg: police and border guards, social security, employment office) to cross information from various sources (data-mining) is crucial in particular in the course of the pre-investigative phase.'

The specific recommendation no 2 is that:

> 'Member States should have in place a procedure based on legislation/regulation allowing security services to have access to law enforcement and relevant government agencies/bodies' databases. This access would be strictly restricted to the need to know and should respect data protection requirements.'

Exactly how can 'data protection requirements' be respected when it is unlikely the individual(s) will know they are under surveillance unless they are later charged? For those not charged but 'caught up in the surveillance net', data protection is meaningless as they will not know their activities are being watched or how 'intelligence' gleaned is used or passed on.

Recommendation no. 3 deals directly with 'Intelligence as evidence in court' which sets out the 'need', recognises that this may affect fundamental rights, but does not deal with the consequences on the rights of defendants and the rule of law. The commentary opens by saying that:

> 'In most Member States intelligence information and in particular covertly obtained intelligence are not admissible as such for use in judicial proceedings.'

He recognises that security services are 'reluctant' for 'intelligence information' to be used in court because this could lead to the 'identification of sources' and the 'disclosure of certain special techniques'. A 'key point' is the:

> 'disclosure of information to the judge and the defence'

and could mean that the:

> 'security service members will have personally to testify in court as privileged witnesses in the framework of an open or closed session etc.'

It might be observed that there is a big difference for fundamental rights whether such evidence is heard in 'open or closed session', whether 'information' is disclosed to the defence lawyer and the defendant, and whether they are allowed to cross-examine.

For de Vries the issue is that 'intelligence' information means an 'enhanced capacity to reinforce criminal investigations and prosecutions.' This is all the more worrying as his philosophy set out in an earlier evaluation report refers to the need to:

> 'maximise the capacity to collect more and more pieces of intelligence' (doc no: 9876/04).

How might security services select instances to suit their purposes from these 'pieces of intelligence' to present to a court? Would a court be able to ask what other surveillance was carried out and what did it show?

He calls for the development of:

> 'a coherent set of laws and procedures to deal with the interaction of intelligence information and the judicial system while respecting fundamental human rights'.

In Recommendation no 3 de Vries says in view of the 'undoubtedly... positive impact' of using intelligence information in court, member states should take 'any necessary steps where needed'. As to fundamental rights he says that an 'evaluation' could:

> 'build on the current works in some Member States as well as in other fora (eg: the G8).'

In other words, the 'solution' found by 'some Member States' (eg: the United Kingdom) and 'G8' to balance the:

> 'civil rights of the individual and the rights and obligations of the state to protect citizens'

is a way of identifying 'best practices'.

Mr de Vries does not argue the case for the legalisation of 'special techniques' for intelligence gathering, he simply says that in some Member States there is 'appropriate legal basis' and under Recommendation 4 says:

> 'Member States should provide security services with appropriate legal basis for the use of special techniques for intelligence gathering.'

Here is no mention of protecting fundamental human rights – presumably because he does not think there is a problem. Recommendation 5 backs the focus on 'recruitment and radicalisation'. Recommendation no 6 is on 'suspect persons and potential perpetrators'. Information should be exchanged on:

> 'persons to be deported, suspect persons that have been trained and suspect persons travelling to or coming from sensitive regions.'

The concept of a 'suspect person' is not defined and can only be taken to mean a person who has 'come to the notice' of the security service or law enforcement agencies. To place under surveillance someone who is known to have been 'trained' to carry out terrorist acts is one thing, but people can be deported for many reasons quite unconnected with terrorism. Moreover, it might be asked: is a person a suspect if they attend a mosque where 'radical' views are expressed and who then travels to a 'sensitive region'?

Security services 'should deepen and widen the exchange of information' on suspect persons (and potential perpetrators) and, in the light of 'ongoing works within the G8', the European Union should continue to discuss how this exchange can be improved – whether within the European Union or with G8 countries is not clear.[46]

Recommendation no 7 refers to Europol's role in 'ongoing investigations' and the problem of the police having to get the permission of a prosecutor to pass over information. He proposes that an *ad hoc* working group be created to overcome 'obstacles'. Recognising that security services are reluctant to give information to Europol, he sees the establishment of 'a security service dimension within SitCen' as the solution.[47] Border controls and the new European Border Agency are another essential aspect of 'gathering and systematic intelligence sharing with law enforcement bodies and security services'.

Mr de Vries makes a number of 'suggestions' which include member states with a 'Muslim community' giving 'support to moderate Islam (and the promotion of intercultural dialogue) ... as a part of a national counter terrorism programme'.

Few of the Recommendations by de Vries are in the adopted Action Plan. However, part of his role is to put, or keep, major issues on the table. It is noteworthy that the Coordinator largely ignores the differences within the European Union member states in their replies to the questionnaire. Issues on which there is a determination within the General Secretariat (especially when backed by key member states and discussions in international fora) are often kept alive and then pushed through.

At an 'informal High Level European Union–United States Freedom, Security and Justice meeting' in Luxembourg on 13-14 January 2005 the 'treatment of classified information in criminal proceedings' was discussed.[48] ('High-Level' means a meeting of top officials from both sides). The 'Outcomes' of the meeting says that:

> 'The meeting addressed the difficulty of using security intelligence on alleged terrorists if the source of this intelligence cannot be disclosed in courts. The Presidency will invite Member States to answer as soon as possible the questionnaire drawn up in the G8 context. The United States offered to submit a paper outlining what the obstacles are and how they could be overcome. The European Union side will then consider the possibility of involving Eurojust and national policy-makers in a workshop on this issue, which is seen by the United States as vital for the credibility of counter-terrorism.'

The proposal first mooted in 2002 and now backed by the United States, United Kingdom, G8, European Union-United States Dromoland Declaration, and the

## Council of Europe: Draft Convention

It is not surprising that these far-ranging developments are echoed in the Council of Europe (CoE, 45 member states). After 11 September 2001, the Council of Europe set up a Multidisciplinary Legal Group on International Action against Terrorism (GMT). Its final report, in November 2002, set out a number of priorities including research on the concepts of *'apologie du terrorisme'* and 'incitement to terrorism'. The research project was published on 24 June 2004.[49] It noted that whereas incitement to commit a criminal offence is common in the member states, *apologie* of a crime is not. The project used a questionnaire to compile an analysis of the law in the Council of Europe and defined *'apologie du terrorisme'* as:

> 'the public expression of praise, support or justification of terrorists and/or terrorist acts'.

Of the forty-five states only eight replies met the criteria that their national legislation defined *'apologie du terrorisme'* and/or 'incitement to terrorism' as a specific criminal offence – these were Bulgaria, Denmark, France, Hungary, Spain, United Kingdom, Italy and Switzerland. Only three states mentioned *'apologie du terrorisme'* as a specific crime – Denmark, France and Spain (Belgium said it intended to). A number of states raised the problem of free expression and freedom of the press if *'apologie du terrorisme'* were to become a crime.

In parallel, in February 2003, the Committee of Ministers set up an 'ad hoc Committee of Experts on Terrorism' with the acronym CODEXTER to implement the priorities of *'apologie du terrorisme'* and 'incitement to terrorism'. CODEXTER is working on a Draft Convention on the prevention of terrorism the latest version of which is dated 14 January 2005.[50] The scope is set out in Article 4.1 which says that:

> 'For the purpose of this Convention, "public provocation to commit an act of terrorism" means the distribution, or otherwise making publicly available, of a message to the public, with the intent to incite the commission of an act of terrorism, including where the message, although not directly advocating such acts, would be reasonably interpreted to have that effect, inter alia, by presenting an act of terrorism as necessary and justified'.

Article 4.2 says a criminal offence as defined in 4.1 should be adopted in domestic law when committed unlawfully and intentionally provided that: 'the provocation causes an imminent danger or likelihood of one or more terrorist acts being committed'. A footnote to Article 4.1 says:

> 'The CODEXTER considered a proposal to include the "terrorist motive" in Articles 4-6 as follows: which has the purpose by its nature or context to intimidate a population or to compel a government or an international organisation to do or abstain from doing any act.
>
> The CODEXTER will revert to this issue on second reading' (footnote 15 referring back to footnote 3).

Articles 4 and 5 cover recruitment and training for terrorism. Article 7 sets out 'ancillary offences' where it would be a criminal offence if a person 'participates as an accomplice' in Articles 4-6 or 'organises or directs others to commit an offence' under these Articles.

The European Union's Action Plan on terrorism (December 2004) records its support for this initiative which includes 'criminalisation of public provocation to commit acts of terrorism' (point 1.3.1). Although the European Union is taking part in CODEXTER, a meeting of Justice and Home Affairs Counsellors (experts on justice and home affairs based in the permanent representatives office of each member state in Brussels) in March recorded that 'the vast majority of delegations were sceptical as to a comprehensive convention against terrorism of the Council of Europe' and 'preferred to focus, at present, on the United Nations work in this field'[51]

However, as the year progressed the Netherlands Council Presidency and now that of Luxembourg is taking a more proactive approach by seeking to establish a European Union member states 'position' on a number of issues. A report from the Luxembourg Presidency at the end of January 2005 refers to discussions in the European Union's Multidisciplinary Group on Organised Crime (CODEXTER experts).[52] First, there appears to be a disagreement among member states on the inclusion of the United Nations Convention on the Suppression of the Financing of Terrorism. The Presidency is recommending keeping it in, while several member states are 'concerned' that:

> 'the inclusion of that convention would lead to a criminalisation of preparatory acts (e.g. public provocation) to a preparatory act (financing) to a preparatory act of the actual "act of terrorism". These Member States regard such a criminalisation as too far reaching.'

A later report, on 4 February, takes up the primary definition in Article 4.1.[53] A majority of European Union governments accept the definition as drafted. However, 'several delegations' wanted to delete the following words at the end: 'by presenting an act of terrorism as necessary and justified', which would be a definite improvement. The result of the discussion was a fudge. The majority position held subject to the addition of a new point 7 in the preamble: 'Recognising that this Convention is not intended to affect established principles relating to freedom of expression and freedom of association in national legal systems.'

Whereas the research study in 2004 showed only three European Union member states had a law akin to *apologie*, now the majority of them are in favour of such a law. Like the Council of Europe's Cyber Crime Convention this one is open to non-Council states to sign up to. During the latter stages of the discussions on the Cyber Crime Convention, the United States joined in and a number of highly retrogressive changes were made.

## Conclusions and implications

As a result of the judgment in the United Kingdom House of Lords Court of Appeal on 16 December 2004 – which declared that indefinite detention without trial was unlawful – the United Kingdom government is to bring forward new legislation. This followed the appeal by 12 men held in Belmarsh high security prison in south

London and Woodhill prison under the Anti-Terrorism, Crime and Security Act 2001 (ATCSA 2001). Lord Hoffman, one of the nine judges, said that:

> 'The real threat to the life of the nation... comes not from terrorism but from laws such as these.'

The use of 'intelligence information' in court or in 'intelligence assessments' for issuing 'control orders'– against people for whom there is insufficient evidence to bring criminal charges – would bring fundamental changes to any normal concept of criminal justice systems in democracies. It could herald, as in the United Kingdom, vetted defence lawyers, refusal to let defendants know the evidence against them, *in camera* (closed) court session, the use of 'intelligence information' from third countries where it will be impossible to question the source, or whether the 'information' had been obtained as a result of torture or ill-treatment or 'rendition'.[54]

The demand for these changes needs to be seen in context. Since 11 September 2001 the European Union has adopted measures to introduce its own passenger name record scheme recording the movements of all third country nationals who enter as well as the external movements of European Union citizens; agreed on the introduction of biometric passports and a huge database carrying personal details; and is planning to introduce the mandatory retention by service providers of all communications traffic data. These measures have little to do with combating terrorism but together seek to make available to the law enforcement and security agencies a mass of personal data over which there are few, if any, controls as to its use.[55] In terms of tackling terrorism there will simply be a bigger and bigger 'haystack' in which to find the same number of 'needles'.

In addition there are new European Union proposals based on the so-called 'principle of availability' agreed under the European Union's 'Hague Programme' on justice and home affairs.[56] This means that if information on a person is held in one agency in a European Union member state, then it can be accessed by any other agency in any other member state. There is also another new 'principle' being put forward by the European Commissioner's Director-General, Mr Frattini, who says there is a need for a 'principle that information may be passed on with the prior consent of the party forwarding it'. This is to enable the passing of personal data to a third state such as the United States, and the 'prior consent' is not that of the individual concerned but the agency which gathered it. It is impossible to control who has access to data in, for example, the United States, which has over 1,500 agencies.[57] What may be a supposition or speculation about an individual's activities in one state may be added to or interpreted quite differently in another.

## – widening the net

The Council of the European Union has reached 'political agreement' on a 'Council Decision on the exchange of information and cooperation concerning terrorist offences'. This envisages in Article 2.1 the exchange of 'information during investigations and prosecutions concerning terrorist offences as set out in Article 1 to 3 of the 2002 Framework Decision on combating terrorism.[58] The 'information' is to be communicated to Europol and Eurojust (European Union prosecutors) and made *'accessible as soon as possible to the authorities of other interested Member States'*. It is sensible that such information should be made available. However, the proposal contains no provision for the 'information' to be removed/deleted should a person be found innocent. There is no provision for the 'information' passed over on those caught up in a 'criminal investigation' but never charged or convicted to be removed/deleted. This is especially worrying as an 'investigation' into a suspected terrorist offence would embrace not just the subject but their family, friends and work and social associates to see if there were any links to the suspected offence. A typical investigation could involve 20-40 other people who are found to be quite innocent but 'information' on them could be 'accessible' to dozens of agencies across the 25 European Union member states.

In April 2004, ten Muslim 'suspects' were arrested and held for questioning in the north of England but were never charged – this could have led to several hundred names and personal details being put into European Union-wide circulation, with no obligation for this data to be deleted. If there is no obligation to delete the names and details of innocent people, they could find themselves on 'watch-lists' for years to come.

There is another problem with the draft Decision. The intention is to widen the scope from those persons, groups and entities placed on updated lists of terrorist groups on formally adopted European Union lists to all those investigated under Articles 1 to 3 of the controversial Framework Decision on combating terrorism (2002) which, despite some amendment, is still ambiguous as to where the line is drawn between terrorism and large-scale protests. It covers, for example, those acting with the aim of:

> 'unduly compelling a Government or international organisation to perform or abstain from performing any act' (Art 1.ii)

To broaden the scope of cooperation on terrorism in this way opens the way for abuse and its application to non-terrorist offences.

### – *the effects of gathering intelligence through 'special investigative techniques'*
Of direct relevance to the use of 'intelligence information' in courts is the legalisation of 'special investigative techniques' (eg: tapping and bugging), techniques the use of which in the past – because they are intrusive, covert and open to abuse – has been limited and very strictly controlled (usually requiring authorisation by a court).

From the 'security' perspective, measures and practices are being introduced to track peoples' movements, to data-mine public and commercial databases, retain and search all telecommunications, create 'watch-lists', infiltrate undercover agents in suspect groups and to recruit informers.[59] Undercover agents and informants inhabit a world of 'hearsay', manipulation and *agent-provocateurs*. Communities, mosques, individuals and groups are targeted for 'disruption' – people are stopped and searched, arrested and released without charge, bank accounts closed without explanation, mysterious burglaries occur, and dissension is encouraged by infiltrators to split and divide groups. Already the security agencies have gathered a mass of 'intelligence' and information on 'suspect' individuals and groups. Many groups and individuals are under 'suspicion' and under surveillance but very few so far have been charged with terrorist offences. In the next phase of the internal 'war on terrorism' the build-up of 'intelligence information' on 'suspected' individuals and groups and targeted communities in European Union states is going to expand enormously.

There are lessons from history when surveillance based on suspicion (rather than investigation leading to trial) becomes the norm. British Irish Rights Watch observed, when commenting on the United Kingdom Prevention of Terrorism Bill, that in Northern Ireland:

> 'Gathering and controlling intelligence took priority over the detection and prevention of crime. The need to recruit, and keep in place, informants meant that some agents were allowed to participate in crimes without being prosecuted, while others were granted *de facto* immunity in order not to blow agents' cover. As a result many people died needlessly in the name of saving lives.'[60]

The use of 'special investigative techniques' aided by undercover agents and informers 'hoovers' up 'intelligence' on specific 'targets' and everyone else who may unknowingly come into contact with them. Such methods carried out covertly and unaccountably (except to the agencies themselves) will lead to an unacceptable intrusion into social and political activity in a democratic society. The lives of the Muslim communities and those who go to mosques to worship become subject to an all pervasive and intrusive surveillance – which, though targeted at potential terrorists, soon extends to all suspected crimes and then to everyday activities.

These practices, techniques and changes in the legal process are, moreover, likely to spill over into the mainstream criminal justice system and establish new norms.[61]

The inexorable logic of the explosion in intelligence-gathering and targeting undertaken by a host of agencies across Europe is that the demands of the law enforcement and security agencies are going to grow for the detention or criminal prosecution of 'suspected' terrorists, 'sympathisers' and 'apologists'. Those who in previous times supported the North Vietnamese and the African National Congress and a host of liberation struggles in the 1960s and 1970s and those today, including the Palestinian struggle, are liable to be caught up in the surveillance 'net'.

Communities which house 'suspect communities' are targeted and subjected to intensive surveillance. Religious and political activity is infiltrated and spied on. And all this is based on the institutionalised racism of post 11 September 2001 –

a racism embedded in the 'politics of fear'.[62] Privacy, accountability, data protection, respect for fundamental rights and democratic norms disappear for those targeted or innocently caught up in the process.

Since 11 September 2001 governments, ministers and officials at all levels of the European Union have maintained that the swathe of new measures introduced have all been 'balanced' as between the needs of security and respect for fundamental rights. Concerned civil society groups across Europe know differently as do refugees, those stopped and searched and detained, and the communities subject to surveillance.[63]

In a democracy when the rights and freedoms of the few are curtailed so, too, are the rights and freedoms of us all.

## References

1 In response to civil liberties critiques the previous Justice and Home Affairs Commissioner in the European Commission, Antonio Vittorino, said:
>'We have not created emergency legislation, we did not create special courts, we did not create special regimes of detention. Those are the areas where real, serious limitations to civil liberties might arise' (launch of the 'Tampere II' process in July 2004).

2 http://www.statewatch.org/news/2005/mar/atcsa-2001-pt-4.htm

3 Privy Counsellors Review Committee:
http://www.statewatch.org/news/2003/dec/16ukguantanamo.htm

4 'Counter-terrorism powers: reconciling security and liberty in an open society' (Cm 6147): http://www.statewatch.org/news/2004/feb/uk-CT-discussion-paper.pdf

5 On 21 July 2004 the parliamentary Joint Committee on Human Rights published a report on the 'option paper': http://www.statewatch.org/news/2004/aug/jt-hum-cttee-terr.htm.pdf and raised some of the issues in the Privy Counsellor Review Committee: Anti-terrorism, Crime and Security Act 2001 Review:
http://www.statewatch.org/news/2003/dec/atcsReport.pdf

6 Judgment on ATCSA 2001, 16.12.04:
http://www.statewatch.org/news/2004/dec/belmarsh-appeal.pdf

7 Statement by the Home Secretary on the introduction of control orders for terrorist 'suspects': http://www.statewatch.org/news/2005/jan/10uk-control-orders.htm

8 Statement on the use of intercepts as evidence:
http://www.statewatch.org/news/2005/jan/11uk-intercepts-evidence.htm

9 UK: Egyptian national 'unlawfully detained' after intervention by Prime Minister: http://www.statewatch.org/news/2004/nov/03blair.htm

10 There appears to be some dispute over how many people could be served control orders. Charles Clarke, the Home Secretary, said that about one hundred could be affected but the Prime Minister says there are over two hundred people who are 'suspected' terrorists in the UK.

11 PTA 2005: http://www.statewatch.org/news/2005/mar/uk-pta-2005.pdf

12 One of the released Belmarsh detainees must under his bail conditions 'remain at all times' in his house, report in by phone five times a day, wear an electronic tag 'at all times', cannot allow anyone else into his house other than his family, lawyer, or 'other such person approved by the Home Office by prior appointment', no computers, mobile phones can be used in his house – which can be searched at any time.

13 Daily Telegraph, 28.1.05.
14 Ben Emmerson's Opinion: http://www.statewatch.org/news/2005/feb/opinion-on-pta-bill.pdf
15 Regulatory Assessment: http://www.statewatch.org/news/2005/mar/pt-bill-reg-assess.pdf
16 http://www.guardian.co.uk/print/0%2C3858%2C5155156-111274%2C00.html
17 He too confuses the issue of 'intercept evidence' and 'intelligence evidence'. The EU's Counter Terrorist Coordinator is on record as saying: 'In most Member States intelligence information and in particular covertly obtained intelligence are not admissible as such for use in judicial proceedings.' (November 2004)
18 In the Home Office statement on the interception of communications (deposited on 26.1.05) it says:
> 'intercept evidence would be unlikely to assist in prosecuting terrorist targets and would not have made a critical difference in supporting criminal prosecution of those detained under ATCSA (Part 4) powers'
19 Court of Appeal, 11 August 2004: http://www.bailii.org/ew/cases/EWCA/Civ/2004/1123.html
20 Travel ban: http://www.guardian.co.uk/print/0,3858,5125522-111274,00.html and the testimony of one of the men: http://observer.guardian.co.uk/print/0,3858,5120738-102285,00.html
21 Statewatch: UK: Anti-terrorist stop & searches target Muslim communities: Report and analysis: http://www.statewatch.org/news/2004/jan/13uk-stop-and-search-targets-Muslim-communites.htm
22 G8 is comprised of the USA, Canada, France, Germany, Italy, the UK, Japan and Russia. The key G8 working groups are the Roma Group (set up in 1978 and comprised of intelligence and internal security officials, known as the Counter Terrorism Experts Group) the Lyon Group (law enforcement officials dealing with organised crime set up in June 1996) and the judicial cooperation group (there are others on issues like immigration).
23 The construction of terrorist lists advanced through the UN, USA and EU was accompanied by measures to track and freeze funding for suspected terrorist groups.
24 On Canada see: http://www.cbc.ca/story/canada/national/2004/12/10/security-certificate-041210.html
25 These were previously known as the 'Lyon Group Recommendations'.
26 EU combating terrorism or crime? http://www.statewatch.org/news/2004/jun/08eu-terrorism-and-crime.htm
27 See survey of current police powers: http://www.statewatch.org/news/2005/feb/01police-data-exchanges.htm
28 'Controlled deliveries' is a relatively recent development and describes a police or customs operation which is deliberately set up by the agencies in order to catch perpetrators.
29 On 25 June 2003 the EU and USA signed agreements on extradition and mutual legal assistance – these have yet to be ratified by the USA and a number of EU member states. The agreement on mutual legal assistance includes the creation of joint investigation teams and requests for 'assistance' – for example, to place under surveillance an individual or group and supply the 'products' of this to the requesting state. See: http://www.statewatch.org/news/2003/apr/01Auseuag.htm
30 Although the UK was not represented at the Dublin meeting, Home Office, police, MI5

and MI6 officials were at the earlier key meetings in G8 of the Roma and Lyon groups. These officials, together with their counterparts from three other EU states (France, Germany and Italy), had by the time of the meeting on 23 February already agreed on the 'concerns', sent out a questionnaire and received replies from all G8 members (including from the UK).

31 EU doc no 6862/04: http://www.statewatch.org/news/2005/jan/6862-eu-us.pdf
32 'Special investigative techniques: http://www.statewatch.org/news/2004/may/G8justice04-legal3.pdf
33 'enhancing the legal framework': http://www.statewatch.org/news/2004/may/G8justice04-legal2.pdf
34 'protecting intelligence': http://www.statewatch.org/news/2004/may/G8justice04-legal4.pdf
35 See, Observer, 19.12.04, article by Martin Bright. It is alleged that one of the men held in Belmarsh prison did exactly this.
36 See, http://www.statewatch.org/news/2004/feb/09gp-guardian.htm
37 Dromoland Declaration: http://www.statewatch.org/news/2005/jan/dromoland-10809.pdf
38 Questionnaire on prevention of terrorism: http://www.statewatch.org/news/2005/jan/eu-g8-10694.pdf
39 It should be noted that the EU-US agreements on extradition and mutual assistance have not yet been formally adopted by the USA. However, such 'mutual cooperation' can take place under existing bilateral agreements.
40 Responses to the questionnaire: http://www.statewatch.org/news/2005/feb/terr-quest-12041.04.pdf
41 A related issue to the use of intelligence in court proceedings is that of freezing or seizing the bank accounts of individuals and groups on terrorist lists. This raises problems when it is used as a 'preventive measure' which has 'led to a series of legal questions' (Council doc no: 14180/3/04):

> *'These questions range from the criteria which should be applied and the evidence which is needed for administrative freezing, the relation of administrative freezing to judicial freezing, seizure and confiscation, to matters of due process, availability of de-listing procedures and the role of intelligence in the designation process.'*

42 Though a reference to the possibility of 'the adoption of legislation for the use of special techniques for intelligence gathering' was slipped into a Presidency Briefing Note given to the press at the Summit.
43 Solana statement: http://www.statewatch.org/news/2004/jun/solana-jha-june-04.pdf See also: Statewatch article: http://www.statewatch.org/news/2005/jan/06sitcen.htm
44 See for example Council doc no: 5670/04, dated 6.2.04, which refers to this concept and gathering details on 'motives for radicalisation within the EU'. The document also suggests looking at 'the Richard Reid/shoe bomb case' and the 'ricin plot in the UK' (which never existed).
45 Council doc no: 14306/3/04: http://www.statewatch.org/news/2005/jan/14306-re03.04-vries.pdf
46 This may be related to discussions with the USA on creating common 'watchlists' or 'red watchlists'.
47 Emergence of SitCen: http://www.statewatch.org/news/2005/jan/06sitcen.htm
48 Informal High-Level EU-US meeting: http://www.statewatch.org/news/2005/feb/eu-us-jan-05-5437.pdf

49 'Apologie du terrorisme' and 'incitement to terrorism': Analytical report: http://www.statewatch.org/news/2005/jan/ribbelink.pdf
50 Draft Convention for the prevention of terrorism, 7.3.05: http://www.statewatch.org/news/2005/mar/coe-draft-con-terrorism-7-march.pdf
51 EU doc no: http://www.statewatch.org/news/2005/jan/7873-04-coe.pdf
52 EU doc no: 5808/05
53 EU doc no: 6049/04
54 'Rendition' is practice carried out by the CIA to send suspected terrorists to be interrogated in countries where the use of torture and ill-treatment has been well documented. CIA prisoners 'tortured' in Arab jails. BBC: http://news.bbc.co.uk/1/hi/programmes/file_on_4/4246089.stm plus Britain accused over CIA's secret torture flights: http://news.independent.co.uk/low_res/story.jsp?story=609538&host=3&dir=506 'Outsourcing torture': http://www.cageprisoners.com/articles.php?aid=5200 and Sweden: Expulsions carried out by US agents, men tortured in Egypt: http://www.statewatch.org/news/2004/oct/05sweden-us-abduction.htm
55 The EU's Joint Supervisory Authorities for Europol, Schengen and Eurojust have told the UK parliament in evidence that recent proposals involve the: *'processing of personal data from different sources on an unprecedented scale'*.
56 'The Hague Programme' on justice and home affairs was agreed by an EU Summit (25 prime ministers) on 5 November 2004. It follows the 'Tampere Programme' adopted in October 1999.
57 Statewatch The 'principle of availability' takes over from the 'notion of privacy': what price data protection?: http://www.statewatch.org/news/2005/feb/07eu-data-prot.htm
58 Statewatch critique: http://www.statewatch.org/news/2002/feb/06Aep.htm
59 In the UK the surveillance of telecommunications is running at an unprecedented level (see Statewatch's Analysis, 1937-2003): http://www.statewatch.org/news/2004/jul/uk-tel-tap-rep-2003.htm In 2003-04 the law enforcement agencies used/had in place 10,409 CHIS (covert human intelligence sources): http://www.statewatch.org/news/2005/mar/chis.pdf and the Special Branch has doubled in size: http://www.statewatch.org/news/2003/sep/01specbranch.htm
60 Briefing February 2005. See also: On the Force Research Unit in Northern Ireland, Statewatch bulletin, vol 13 no 5, and on GAL in Spain, Statewatch bulletin vol 9 no 3.4.
61 Similarly these techniques are being brought to bear on 'normal' police life in the surveillance of protests, especially where people come together from a number of different EU states.
62 'Racism in the age of globalisation', A Sivanandan: http://www.irr.org.uk/2004/october/ha000024.html
63 In a moment of honesty UK Home Secretary, Charles Clarke, when asked about claims that MI6 played an active role in the kidnapping of a Briton who spent 33 months in Guantanamo Bay, responded: *'I'm all in favour of human rights, but I'm even more in favour of our national security being protected'* (Guardian, 7.2.05).

## THE BERTRAND RUSSELL PEACE FOUNDATION
# DOSSIER

### WORLD TRIBUNAL ON IRAQ
### 23-27 JUNE 2005 – ISTANBUL

The World Tribunal on Iraq has been gathering momentum for two years, ever since an initial meeting at the European Parliament in Brussels in May 2003 under the auspices of the European Network for Peace and Human Rights, which was established by the Russell Foundation.

Tribunal sessions have been held in Barcelona, Brussels, Copenhagen, Frankfurt, Geneva, Lisbon, London, Mumbai, New York, Rome, Seoul, Stockholm and Tokyo.

The culminating session of the Tribunal will be held in Istanbul in the grounds of the Topkapi Palace from 23$^{rd}$ to 27$^{th}$ of June. The Tribunal will hear new reports and testimonies, as well as examining the results of previous sessions, and will then reach its decision.

The panel of advocates will include Denis Halliday, who was Assistant to the UN Secretary General and Coordinator of the UN Humanitarian Aid Programme in Iraq, and Scott Ritter, who served as a weapons inspector with the United Nations Special Commission (UNSCOM) in Iraq.

'Taking its cue from the Russell Tribunal of the late 1960s, the World Tribunal on Iraq is aimed at challenging the silence around the aggression against Iraq and seeking the truth about the war and occupation in Iraq,' said Melek Taylan, spokesperson for the Tribunal. 'This will be a process of listening, reflection, evaluation and informed judgment based on concrete evidence.'

The World Tribunal on Iraq is the initiative of a network of local groups worldwide. The project consists of commissions of inquiry and sessions held around the world investigating various issues related to the war on Iraq, such as the legality of the war, the role of the United Nations, war crimes, the role of the media, and the destruction of cultural sites and the environment. People from Iraq, as well as experts and activists from outside the country, gave testimony and presented their reports during these sessions.

'By this Tribunal, we aim to leave a record to history of what actually happened, and how it happened, in Iraq,' says Mrs Taylan. 'We will compile all the evidence in a book. Since the so-called international community is, at the moment, incapable of judging the reasons and the actors responsible for the killings of innocent people in Iraq, the people of the world will take the initiative on its behalf.'

For more information please contact the office of the World Tribunal on Iraq in Istanbul (phone 0090 212 244 7370) or look online (www.worldtribunal.org).

## OIL MOTIVATED WAR ON IRAQ – BLIX

On 7 April 2005, Associated Press reported that Hans Blix, who served as the UN's chief weapons inspector in Iraq, told a Swedish news agency that oil was one of the reasons for the US-led invasion of Iraq.

'I did not think so at first. But the US is incredibly dependent on oil,' said Dr Blix. 'They wanted to secure oil in case competition on the world market becomes too hard.' Blix added that another reason for the invasion was a need to move US troops from Saudi Arabia.

Competition over oil is creating tension between the United States and China, Blix said, suggesting nuclear power as a more environmentally friendly source of energy. 'I believe the greatest threat in the long term is the greenhouse effect,' said Blix.

He defended the United Nations, despite recent scandals including allegations of corruption in the oil-for-food programme for Iraq. 'The criticism is, in my view, a revenge from American political circles for the defeat over Iraq,' Blix was quoted as saying.

## IRAQ'S CO-OPERATION WITH THE WEAPONS INSPECTORS

*Jack Straw strongly criticised the Iraqi Declaration on Weapons of Mass Destruction, submitted in December 2002 in accordance with the requirements of UN Security Council Resolution 1441, on the grounds that it had all been seen before. The Declaration has never been published. Even the majority of Security Council members have seen only a heavily censored version comprising some 4,000 out of a total of 12,000 pages (see Spokesman 77,78,81 and 84). But the Iraqi administration had previously submitted comprehensive information to the Security Council, as can be seen in this statement to the Council by Iraq's Ambassador to the United Nations, Mohammed Aldouri, on 16 October 2002.*

'The scale of the inspection process to which Iraq has submitted indicates co-operation on a large scale: Iraq's implementation of resolution 687 (1991) over the seven years and seven months to 15 December 1998 involved the following:

276 inspection teams, made up of a total of 3,845 inspectors, and 80 delegations in the form of special missions undertook 3,392 visits to Iraqi sites. Among these teams were 94 teams specialising in meetings and interviews, which met for a total of 2,359 hours with 1,378 people connected directly or indirectly with Iraq's previous programmes.

There were 192 monitoring teams involving 1,332 inspectors who undertook 10,256 inspection visits to sites subject to the monitoring system, as well as other sites.

The United Nations Special Commission (UNSCOM) and the International Atomic Energy Agency (IAEA) used 140 surveillance cameras at 29 sites and 30 sensors at 23 sites, as well as 1,929 labels on 1,832 facilities and pieces of equipment in monitoring 161 sites. UNSCOM placed 9,026 labels on 99 types of missile with a range of less than seven kilometres.

UNSCOM and IAEA also undertook 2,967 helicopter sorties in their work, for a total of 4,480 flight hours. The United States undertook 434 U-2 surveillance sorties for a total of 1,800 flight hours. Iraq submitted 1,744,000 pages of documents to UNSCOM and the International Atomic Energy Agency, along with a number of video-tapes and nine kilometres of microfilm, containing 600,000 pictures and 50,000 microfilm slides.'

## GERMANS WANT AMERICAN NUKES TO GO

A poll published by *Der Spiegel* on 2 May 2005 shows that more than three-quarters of Germans want US nuclear weapons withdrawn from Germany. The poll indicates very high support for withdrawal even among supporters of the conservative parties (CDU/CSU). Four out of five supporters of the socialists (SPD) also support removal, as do three out of every five supporters of the Liberal Party (FDP), which recently submitted a resolution in the German Parliament calling for withdrawal of these weapons.

A thousand individuals were asked: 'In Germany there are still 150 nuclear weapons under US command. Should these nuclear weapons be withdrawn from Germany?' The response was:

|     | Overall | CDU/CSU | SPD | Greens | FDP |
|-----|---------|---------|-----|--------|-----|
| Yes | 76      | 73      | 82  | 90     | 66  |
| No  | 18      | 24      | 15  | 5      | 29  |

During a meeting with the German foreign ministry in February, the head of the arms control section said he personally favoured a withdrawal but that there was 'no political pressure' to do so. The poll seems to change that.

On a recent visit to Ramstein air base, Headquarters of the US Air Force Europe, German Defence Minister Peter Struck said 'I'm of the same opinion as Foreign Minister Fischer, that we will have to talk about this issue (nuclear weapons removal) in the appropriate NATO bodies… We will have to clarify this issue in consultation with the other European allies, which still host nuclear weapons on their territory.'

On the same visit, Prime Minister Beck of Rhineland Palatinate said 'I'm in full consensus with the Federal Government, that there is no threat any longer that could justify continuing their (nuclear weaspons) deployment permanently in any way. Therefore, I support endeavours jointly with NATO to remove these weapons.'

## …SO DO THE BELGIANS

On 21 April 2005, the Belgian Senate passed a resolution on nuclear disarmament and non-proliferation which called for the withdrawal of US nuclear weapons based in Europe.

This is the first time that a Parliament in Europe has demanded the withdrawal of the 480 US nuclear weapons based in Belgium, Germany, England, Italy, the Netherlands and Turkey. The United States is the only country which has nuclear weapons stationed on the territory of other countries.

The Senate Commission on Foreign Affairs and Defence approved the resolution in March. It calls on the Belgian government to adopt a balanced approach to nuclear non-proliferation and disarmament. The resolution makes reference to the disarmament obligations contained in Article VI of the Nuclear Non-Proliferation Treaty (NPT). It asks the government to contribute to a stronger disarmament agenda at the NPT Review Conference in New York in May 2005, and to pursue this policy in the European Union and NATO, including taking steps towards the creation of a nuclear weapon free zone formed by all non-nuclear weapons states in Europe.

The resolution was submitted by Senators Patrik Vankrunkelsven (VLD), Lionel Vandenberghe (Spirit), Pierre Galand (PS), Sabine de Bethune (CD&V), Christian Brotcorne (cdH), Annemie Van de Casteele (VLD) and Philippe Mahoux (PS).

## ...AND IN HOLLAND, TOO

A resolution calling for the removal of American nuclear weapons from Europe was tabled in the Netherlands Parliament on 28 April 2005. This was done by three opposition parties: GreenLeft (Farah Karimi), Socialist Party (Krista van Velzen) and the Labour Party (Bert Koenders). Together they have 60 seats in the 150 member parliament. The resolution states:

> 'This Chamber...Considering that a new review conference in the framework of the Non-Proliferation Treaty is taking place in May 2005;
> Is of the opinion that the nuclear weapon states should unreservedly strive to completely eliminate their nuclear arsenals;
> Is of the opinion that in view of the upcoming NPT Review Conference initiatives should be taken for nuclear disarmament and non-proliferation in various international fora, like the NPT Review Conference, NATO and the European Union;
> Requests the government to undertake steps for a strict disarmament agenda, including the withdrawal of all American nuclear weapons from Europe in order to comply with article VI of the Non-Proliferation Treaty...'

# CAMBRIDGE

# ... at the cutting edge

**The Ethics and Politics of Asylum**
Liberal Democracy and the Response to Refugees
Matthew J. Gibney
'This is the only book length study available of the ethics of asylum ... It is intelligent, perceptive, and lucidly written. Anyone interested in questions about refugees should read this book.'
Joseph H. Carens, University of Toronto
£40.00 | HB | 0 521 80417 5 | 298pp
£15.99 | PB | 0 521 00937 5

**Deadly Connections**
States that Sponsor Terrorism
Daniel Byman
'... there is no other current book on the same topic. I learned a tremendous amount by reading it.'
Karin von Hippel, London School of Economics
'Dan Byman has written what will likely become the standard text on state-sponsored terrorism.'
Bruce Hoffman, author of Inside Terrorism and former Director of RAND Corporation, Washington DC
**Publication June 2005**
c.£15.00 | HB | 0 521 83973 4 | 280pp

forthcoming

forthcoming

**The Market for Force**
The Consequences of Privatizing Security
Deborah D. Avant
The first serious attempt to grapple with the difficult trade-offs involved in controlling private security in the global market.
**Publication June 2005**
c.£40.00 | HB | 0 521 85026 6 | 320pp
c.£16.99 | PB | 0 521 61535 6

www.cambridge.org

# CAMBRIDGE UNIVERSITY PRESS

# Reviews

## Dark Times

Karen J. Greenberg and Joshua L. Dratel, *The Torture Papers: The Road to Abu Ghraib*, Cambridge University Press, 1249 pages, hardback ISBN 052185324 9, £27.50
Mark Danner, *Torture and Truth: America, Abu Ghraib and the War on Terror*, Granta Books, 573 pages, paperback ISBN 186207772X, £16.99
Steven Strasser, *The Abu Ghraib Investigations*, Public Affairs, New York, 178 pages, paperback ISBN 1586483196, $14

Porter J. Goss, the new Director of Central Intelligence in the United States, appeared before Congress in March to reassure the legislature that interrogations 'at this time' were all tickety-boo. However, he was not sure, when asked, whether this statement would be valid about previous misdeeds. Now, no techniques of enquiry 'are in any way against the law...or would be considered torture or anything like that', said Mr. Goss. But Mr. Goss could not tell the Senate Armed Services Committee whether the Agency's techniques of interrogation had been 'expanded' after the attacks of September 2001, on the Twin Towers, and the Pentagon. 'I am not able to tell you that' he said, but he 'might be able to elaborate' in closed session when classified testimony was being heard. In any case, there is a Catch 22 which governs Porter Goss' statements, like all others by officialdom in the United States. They are anxious to protest fidelity to American norms, and obedience to the American law. The Geneva Conventions, on the other hand, were formulated by lesser breeds whose law seemed hardly to merit consideration.

Three CIA employees may face criminal prosecutions, in respect of the deaths of prisoners in Afghanistan and Iraq.

A couple of days before Porter Goss' testimony was heard, *The New York Times* reported the deaths of at least twenty-six prisoners in American custody in Afghanistan and Iraq. Eighteen American servicemen have been recommended for prosecution, and eight are still under investigation. One of the deaths occurred in the Abu Ghraib prison. Nine Iraqis had died in the custody of the Marine Corps. No one has volunteered precise details of the circumstances of their deaths. Two soldiers are facing charges of manslaughter at the Bagram facility in Afghanistan.

These three books explain the background circumstances of all such cases. They are composed for the most part of documents. They speak very bluntly and are complemented by the distressing photographs from Abu Ghraib which may enable us to see for ourselves whether the ill-treatment offered to prisoners constitutes torture or not.

*The Torture Papers* offers the most extensive collection of documents, which show how Porter Goss should have answered the question about changes in interrogation practices after 9/11. Blow by blow, this book provides the official reasoning behind the shredding of Geneva Conventions. Deputy Assistant

Attorney General John Yoo offers the President's staff detailed advice on the constitutional authority for the conduct of military operations against terrorists and the nations supporting them. But Mr. Yoo seeks to validate the use of pre-emptive military force 'whether or not' this can be linked to the specific terrorist acts of September 11th. The President 'has the plenary constitutional power to take such military actions as he deems necessary and appropriate to respond to the terrorist attacks upon the United States on September 11th 2001. Force can be used both to retaliate for those attacks, and to prevent and deter future assaults...'.

Following Mr. Yoo's first diktat, Greenberg and Dratel have assembled detailed documentation on the modes of action to prevent detainees from claiming the protection of habeas corpus. On January 9th, Mr. Yoo turned his attention to demolishing the protections of the Geneva Conventions, and to steering the administration through the hazards of the international law governing war crimes. Then this daunting volume shows how coercive interrogation and torture fanned out from Afghanistan through Guantanamo to Abu Ghraib.

The revelations which exploded in the world's press in 2004, showing a pattern of systematic cruelty and ill-treatment of detainees in the former interrogation centre of Saddam Hussein, Abu Ghraib, now under the management of the American military, revealed the logical working out of these executive decisions, from offices in the White House through to the forces on the ground at Camp Bucca, Camp Ashraf, Abu Ghraib, and the high valued detainee complex at Camp Cropper.

Lieutenant General Ricardo S. Sanchez set up an enquiry into reports of detainee abuse, escapes from confinement facilities, and lapses of accountability. Antonio M. Taguba was charged with the conduct of this investigation. His long report, in dry officialese, takes up many pages of this volume, and is strongly featured in the other two books under review.

Taguba found that

'The intentional abuse of detainees by military police personnel included the following acts:

(a) punching, slapping and kicking detainees, jumping on their naked feet;
(b) videotaping and photographing naked male and female detainees;
(c) forcibly arranging detainees in various sexually explicit positions for photographing;
(d) forcing detainees to remove their clothing and keeping them naked for several days at a time;
(e) forcing naked male detainees to wear women's underwear;
(f) forcing groups of male detainees to masturbate themselves while being photographed and videotaped;
(g) arranging naked male detainees in a pile and then jumping on them;
(h) positioning a naked detainee on a meal ready-to-eat (MRE) box, with a sandbag on his head, and attaching wires to his fingers, toes and penis to simulate electric torture;
(i) writing "I am a rapest" (sic) on the leg of a detainee alleged to have forcibly raped a 15 year old fellow detainee, and then photographing him naked;
(j) placing a dog chain or strap around a naked detainees neck and having a female soldier pose for a picture;

(k) a male MP guard having sex with a female detainee;
(l) using military working dogs (without muzzles) to intimidate and frighten detainees, and in at least one case biting and severely injuring a detainee;
(m) taking photographs of dead Iraqi detainees.'

Taguba goes on to offer detailed evidence in support of these allegations, and his report includes witness statements which are predictably forbidding. Some documents featured here have been published in whole or in part in the press. We have featured a number of them in previous issues of *The Spokesman*, including, notably, the report of the International Committee of the Red Cross (see *Spokesman 82)*.

Responsible American political leaders expressed their horror at this kind of allegation, and there was a small flood of complaints to the authorities, some of which are featured here.

Mark Danner has conveniently republished five essays explaining the case, from the *New York Review of Books* and the *New Yorker*, which demonstrate how President Bush thought himself to be outside the scope of international law. What the Americans later did at Abu Ghraib followed inexorably from their deeds in Afghanistan at Bagram, and later at Guantanamo. Once again, he reiterates that prisoners were systematically abused, beaten, threatened by slavering dogs, and anally raped with sticks and other objects.

Steven Strasser's more tightly edited account of these events focuses on the summary of abuses at Abu Ghraib. A catalogue of physical abuses includes forcing an internee to stand while handcuffed in such a way as to dislocate his shoulder. The deployment of dogs was clearly meant to spread terror. Two boys had a dog thrust into their cell. Both of them 'were screaming and crying, with the youngest and smallest trying to hide behind the other'. Major General George R. Fry investigated allegations involving detainee abuse, sixteen of which were, or were said to have been 'requested, encouraged, condoned or solicited by military intelligence personnel. The abuse, however, was directed on an individual basis, and never officially sanctioned or approved'. In eleven cases military intelligence was found to be directly involved in the abuse.

Students of these three distressing books may very well come to agree that they record the deeds of a number of bad apples, concentrated in the vicinity of the White House, and the higher reaches of the military.

How far were American fashions imitated by their British followers? This marks out an interesting field of enquiry. What is already very clear is that the British Government greeted critical reports from the International Committee of the Red Cross with a singular lack of curiosity. In their ponderously empirical style, the British were reluctant to offer general codes of guidance. Instead, they failed to read the offending reports, and ensured that they remained on the desks of subalterns, beneath the reach of the men of authority.

Yes, there is a long history of torture. But the whole history of civilisation has been marked out by the developing understanding that torture is unacceptable, abhorrent, a defilement of all who engage in it.

Do Tony Blair and Jack Straw fail the torture test? There is an uncomfortable body of evidence which suggests that they may indeed.

*Ken Coates*

## Peace Activist

Mary-Louise Engels, *Rosalie Bertell: Scientist, Eco-Feminist, Visionary*, Women's Press, Canada, paperback ISBN 0889614504, Canadian $19.95, US $12.95

Rosalie Bertell has been a hero of mine for many years, so I was pleased to learn that a much needed biography of her was in the making. I was even more pleased to be asked to contribute some thoughts and a photo of Rosalie to Engels' work. The scholarship, courage, determination and foresight of this remarkable woman deserve to be known to all activists seeking sources of inspiration and wisdom.

Frail from birth, Rosalie was a serious student encouraged in her talent for mathematics and music by caring parents. Her Canadian mother was her inspiration and active supporter in social action. From her American father – the inventor of the car night mirror – she developed her scientific and practical abilities. Rosalie knew from a young age that she would enter a convent and take the religious life, much as she enjoyed her home, school and social life. She was in her teens at the end of World War Two and the war 'challenged her beliefs about the goodness of the universe…the victory achieved through atomic fire in Japan raised questions that would preoccupy her throughout her life.' Rosalie believes that the war never ended – that post-World War Two, the United States and most of the world continue to arm and create a permanent war economy and mentality.

After a period in a Carmelite convent where she learned that women can develop all the practical skills for existence, Rosalie's health failed again and she returned to secular life. Her studies continued and she gained a doctorate (critics love to call her Sister Bertell, just a woman and a nun, not a real scientist.) Her concerns about the unleashing of atomic energy and weaponry on the world continued in her research and teaching career; she did original and groundbreaking work connecting cancer to nuclear installations and low-level radiation. She joined the Grey Nuns, an order with an historic tradition of social service.

Everything Rosalie has done in her career as a scientist and an activist has been illuminated by her concern for the health of humanity and all life forms, and the destructive effects of radioactivity. She became an advocate for community groups opposing nuclear development in the United States and Canada. She travelled the world to see, study and inform the public about the effects of the nuclear industry and bomb testing. Her work has always shown her support for groups that were more vulnerable and threatened by radiation than others: women and children; aboriginal and majority world peoples; world workers in uranium mines and nuclear facilities.

Eventually she became too successful; her willingness to oppose the white male nuclear establishment brought on pressure at her workplaces and many public attacks; she chose to become an independent consultant. When her life was threatened in a highway 'accident', she moved to Canada, where she still maintains citizenship. In 2004 she was anxious to cast her vote in the Canadian federal election, even though by then she had returned to the United States and was recovering from surgery.

During her twenty years in Canada her work became more accepted – unfortunately many of her predictions came true. She set up an Institute for international health to support her work and continued her extensive, often gruelling, travels. She received many awards, including the Right Livelihood Award from Sweden with her co-researcher Alice Stuart of the United Kingdom. She has written several books and her most recent, *Planet Earth: The latest weapon of war,* is the culmination of her experience as a researcher and activist. She sees that our relentless blind militarisation is the greatest threat to the earth's environment and life. Rosalie is still working, accepting of and coping with her physical frailty, gaining strength from her religious life and a world of supporters. Much of her present work deals with the use and effects of 'depleted uranium', another hideous weapon of war.

In *Planet Earth* Rosalie is optimistic about the possibility for change. She points out that our society has changed its core values – also attitudes and legislation – on many issues from women's rights, children's rights, animal welfare and homosexual rights. She believes we can and will change our values about militarisation. She works with many people and groups, always generous with her time and wisdom. In Beijing at the UN Women's Forum she called on us to be responsible gatherers and transmitters of information and knowledge. 'We Can Be Our Own Media'.

I have been honoured to have Rosalie's friendship for many years and I often quote her in my writing and speeches, referring to her science and her faith in human betterment. I gain courage from her passion to be 'fruitful', and her encouragement to others to stand up for life.

Engels' biography gives a comprehensive and easily understood chronology of the basis of Rosalie's scientific research and she shows how Rosalie illustrates the possibility of a fulfilled life as a scientist and an activist outside the mainstream establishment – something many of us hope to achieve. If I ever do, it will be with the guidance of Rosalie.

The last words in this book and this review are by Rosalie Bertell herself. 'The continuity of life, the call for making things better for the next and the next generations blots out all hesitation…We have to be part of something larger than ourselves, because our dreams are often bigger than our lifetimes.'

*Theresa Wolfwood*

## Towering Collection

***Frederick Engels Letters 1892-95, Marx and Engels Collected Works**, Volume 50, Lawrence and Wishart, 640 pages, £45*

Frederick Engels died in July 1895. His ashes were scattered off Beachy Head, but his prodigious correspondence was preserved, and brings to a culmination this towering collection of his works and those of Karl Marx. This is the 50$^{th}$ volume in the series, which has been painstakingly edited under the auspices of three commissions of scholars, from Britain, the United States and Russia.

The convulsive changes in our present times saw this series begun with the collaboration of the Institute of Marxism Leninism, which is now the Russian Independent Institute of Social and National Problems. But in spite of the name changes, the care taken with these volumes has been persistent, indeed exemplary.

The first three volumes included all the surviving juvenilia of Marx, from his thoughts on choosing a profession to an early letter to his father. They ranged from his doctoral dissertation on differences between the Democritean and Epicurean philosophy of nature to his earliest political writings in the newspaper *Rheinische Zeitung*. Engels made his first appearance in the second volume with a poem on the Bedouin, written and first published in 1838. By the time of the fourth volume, the collaboration of the two men had begun in earnest with their long and difficult book on *The Holy Family*, criticising Bruno Bauer and others. By 1844 Engels was engaged on his work on *The Condition of the Working Class in England*, which still remains as vivid as it was a century and a half ago, and disconcertingly contemporary to boot.

The next volumes contain the general writing, books and articles, on all the political themes which were addressed by Marx and Engels. Following, from volume 30 to 37, looms the mighty edifice of *Capital*, and all the economic writings which accompanied it. Thereafter, volumes 38 to 50 cover the correspondence of both men, which is not only vast, but also encyclopaedic: a vital history of the beginnings of the Socialist movement, from which many more histories are still to be quarried. There were almost four thousand letters, well over half of which were published for the first time in English in this edition.

No good library in the civilised world will be complete without this Collection. It is not only a treasure house for all those with an interest in Marx, but its significance will grow as these men speak more and more intimately in their own voices, without the benefit of the accretions of various official isms.

\* \* \*

This final 50$^{th}$ volume winds up the series with 320 letters from Engels, most of which have not formerly appeared in English. Much attention is given to questions of peace and war, and to the attitudes of the nascent Socialist movement to the growing threat of global conflict. Engels laboured under the dawning certainty that 'the next war, if it comes at all, will not permit of being localised in any way'.

Vast armies were being assembled, and Europe was preparing for the long descent into the bloodlust of the next century. The new Socialists were beginning a series of programmatic discussions, pamphlets and theses on disarmament.

The list of Engels' correspondents during his last few years amounts to a veritable directory of European Socialism, from Pablo Iglesias in Spain, through to Georgi Plekhanov in Russia. Kautsky, Bernstein, Adler, and Bebel, of course, provide an axis of commitment in this correspondence, and reflect the trials and triumphs of German social democracy.

From the troubles of thought in ancient Greece, through to the squabbles of the founders of twentieth century Socialism, these are books with a profound humanity, resonant in their optimism, firmly proclaiming an agenda which is not completed, and certainly not in any way concluded.

*Ken Coates*

## Kansas

**Thomas Frank, *What's the Matter with America? The Resistible Rise of the American Right*, Secker & Warburg, 306 pages, paperback ISBN 0436205394 £12**

This US best seller, offered in the UK at a ridiculous price, was published in 2004 in the United States under the title *What's the Matter with Kansas?* The US title was entirely appropriate since Frank bases his whole story on the state he was brought up in, which lies in the mid-West on the Missouri at the very heart of the United States, physically, socially and politically. Kansas lies on a dry plain, hot as hell in the summer and cold in the winter. Its history is of the pioneers who went West to farm lands that the railways opened up. The settlers were Puritan, abolitionists, hard working, clannish and politically radical. Kansas spawned socialists like Eugene Debs, fiery progressives like La Folette, the Industrial Workers of the World (IWW), and trade union organisers like Walter Reuther. Kansas became a meat-packing centre, and then cheap labour off the land found employment in the Boeing and other aircraft factories. Much of this work has now gone elsewhere and Kansas is today the poorest state in America with the highest unemployment. And its citizens voted more solidly for Bush than those of any other state. How could that be?

In this book Thomas Frank seeks to give the answer in terms of what he calls the conservative 'backlash'. In the decline of their state Kansans feel rejected and hold it against those whom they see as their class enemy, not the great capitalist corporations that are their real oppressors but the liberal élite. For the economic element has somehow been taken out of class and only the culture remains. So in the recent election George Bush appears as the simple farm boy from Texas, a born again Christian who has mended his ways, notwithstanding his Harvard education and millions of oil money. Kerry by contrast was the very exemplar of the liberal élite with his Bostonian accent and arrogant academic speechifying. What has caused the destruction of a once happy Middle West community, it is believed, is the undermining of its moral certainties by the permissive, loose living, spendthrift ways of the professional intelligentsia, debauching their children with the profligacy of opinions. They can see it on the television programmes and in the films and the reports of all the think tanks in the magazines and papers they read.

So what do they do? They turn back to their old religious certainties and take up all the causes that the liberals have abandoned – creationism, pro-life campaigns, the taboo on homosexuals, the holiness of marriage and unholiness of single sex marriages and of pre-marital intercourse, prohibition, the right to own a gun, the death penalty. Fundamentalism in religion encourages a positive crusade against liberal immorality in its Godless education, playing with life in stem cell research, gun laws and welfarism. It is beyond belief that those who will suffer most from tax cuts for the rich and cuts in public spending for the poor are the same who will argue and voted for the very measures that will have that effect.

Frank gives extraordinary and even amusing detailed accounts of the campaigns in Kansas for every kind of illiberal and antediluvian cause.

This is all the result, according to Frank, of the conservative backlash against the New Deal, trade union power and big government. It is a convincing story, except for the fact that far too little importance is granted by him to the failure of the Democrats to defend their natural constituencies among the blue collar workers, the blacks and Hispanic immigrants. Howard Dean, who tried, is only mentioned once by Frank in a telling footnote on page 17, which is designed to illustrate how Kansans think about Vermont, the New England State of which Howard Dean had been the Governor. In a commercial TV show, aired in early 2004 by the conservative Club for Growth, two supposedly average people advised Dean 'to take his tax-hiking, government spending, latte drinking, sushi eating, Volvo driving, *New York Times*-reading, body piercing, Hollywood-loving, left-wing freak show back to Vermont, where it belongs' . That really says it all.

*Michael Barratt Brown*

## Celebrating the Empire

**Caroline Elkins, *Britain's Gulag: The Brutal End of Empire in Kenya*, Jonathan Cape, 352 pages, hardback ISBN 022407363X, £20**

> '…On the third day of his four-nation African tour, the Chancellor made a discreet dawn visit to Dar es Salaam's small Commonwealth Cemetery, where he laid a wreath in honour of foreign servicemen. Surrounded by the impeccably tended graves of more than three hundred soldiers of the Empire, Mr. Brown said Britain no longer had to make excuses for its record, as a colonial power.
> 
> …Speaking to the *Daily Mail*, he said:
> "I have talked to many people on my visit to Africa and the days of Britain having to apologise for its colonial history are over."'

Gordon Brown was echoing the thoughts of a small, if disreputable, group of scholars, who have rediscovered the Empire as a fount of sweetness and light.

Recently, some of these personages have stepped outside the groves of academe, to advise the Prime Minister, or install themselves in the ample secretariat of Mr. Solana.

Now Caroline Elkins steps forward to spoil all this mood music with a splendidly, heroically, discordant note. She has dedicated herself to recovering the forgotten savagery of the war against the Mau Mau in Kenya, and the determined ruthlessness of the British occupation.

Years before, some Kikuyu had offered resistance to the British intrusion in East Africa, which became more resolute at the beginning of the Century, after the completion of the Uganda railway. This was an engineering miracle aimed at preventing feared German efforts to seize and dam the headwaters of the Nile. This railway thus received the nickname: the Lunatic Express, and it attracted appropriate criticism in the metropolitan power. So it became urgent to find a reliable group of settlers to develop the colony's production, to use the new railway for export and to pay back the lavish investment that already seemed to have been so wasteful.

> 'Settlers in Kenya' reads a contemporary advertisement, 'Britain's next and most attractive colony. Low prices at present for fertile areas. No richer soil in the British Empire. Kenya colony makes a practical appeal to the intending settler with some capital. Its valuable crops give high yields due to the high fertility of the soil, adequate rainfall and abundant sunshine. Secure the advantage of native labour to supplement your own effort.'

The native labour was not, however, universally enthusiastic about this, and soon one British officer gave it as his opinion that 'there is only one way of improving the Wakikuyu – that is wipe them out'.

Gordon Brown could read Ms Elkins chapter on the Pax Britannica with some profit, although today's Pax Americana may have already drawn lessons more to his liking. Now white settlers are not the fashionable tools of subjugation. That this has been recognised is not a result of the civilising mission, but of the fierce resistance of the Kikuyu. After the Second World War (for freedom) it was not too surprising that over the whole area in Kenya, a million and a half people rose up in arms, to insist on the return of their lands, and of their own freedom. The British colonial government detained almost the entire population, keeping them in camps or confining them to their villages, and separating their enclosures with barbed wire. From 1952 until the war ended in 1960, thousands of detainees died from disease, starvation, and the effects of systematic brutality. The author estimates that the mortality could have reached one hundred thousand or more.

Mau Mau suspects were represented as bestial savages, so that it was deemed perfectly reasonable to hook them up to generators and electrocute them, or to tie them to the back of Land Rovers, and drive off, making them run until they dropped, and then dragging them behind until they fell to bits. This kind of education was performed in front of large groups of Mau Mau suspects, in order to teach them that it might be wise to collaborate with the authorities. As the necessary lessons took too long to learn, there were mass shootings and other more brutal detentions.

Caroline Elkins has interviewed survivors, and the relatives of people who perished, and has compiled a searing account of the prolonged repression. The British authorities were rigorous and scientific in covering their tracks, and after the fall of the colonial occupation there were systematic attempts to eliminate the records. No doubt this made it easier for a future Chancellor to invite us all to forget. But readers of this powerful book will not find much for the British occupation to celebrate.

*John Pearce*

## Incomers

**Barry Pilton, *The Valley*, Bloomsbury, 288 pages, paperback ISBN 0747571686 £10**

If you have ever found yourself trying to adjust as an 'incomer' to a closed rural community in a remote part of Yorkshire or Scotland or southern Spain or the Algarve, this is the book for you. If you have actually thought of settling there, in retirement for example, this book will warn you not to waste your money. If you just want a succession of belly laughs at the impenetrable resistance that such attempts at adjustment evoke in one beautifully imagined situation, then read the book for the sheer fun of the thing. The script writer Barry Pilton has set his first novel in what he calls 'Mid-Wales', as if the country had extremities but only an unexplored middle. The local characters are beautifully drawn – Dafydd the Post, who is in constant fear of his 'assessment'; Gwillim the cowman who unwillingly keeps the only pub in his spare time; Gareth the shepherd whose Irish wife's long legs seduce the local bank manager; Teg and Beg, the mole catchers; the 'Windowman', who doesn't like making windows; Eryl the disinherited land owner; the local reporter Clydog 'the Knowledge', and many others. All have their own irresistible response to the incomers. These consist of an artistic hippy couple and a businessman of Georgian descent, who has inherited the land and the big house and tries, without success, to bring the valley into the modern world. The only book to compare with this is Robin Jenkins's superb study of the Algarve, *The Road to Alto*. That is a serious sociological study. *The Valley* is to be read for the laughs, but it is based on some perceptive social observation.

*MBB*